PRAISE FOR *EVEREST STRONG*

"Motivation is the key with any challenge, and Rob Besecker has plenty, as he depicts in this amazing adventure. Having had the pleasure of meeting Rob in Antarctica in 2010, I'm happy to see his aspirations come to completion as he continues to move onward and upward here in *Everest Strong*."

—**PETER HILLARY**, mountaineer, son of Sir Edmund Hillary, and coauthor of *In the Ghost Country: A Lifetime Spent on the Edge*

"*Everest Strong* is a story that reminds us all that when we have willpower and determination, we are able to accomplish our goals despite what life has given us. Rob Besecker has shown us that it is possible to accomplish anything if you are passionate about what you want to achieve. There is no summit that is too high to achieve. Climb high and climb on!"

—**JAMLING TENZING NORGAY**, mountaineer, son of Tenzing Norgay Sherpa, and author of *Touching My Father's Soul: A Sherpa's Journey to the Top of Everest*

"*Everest Strong* is compelling, raw, and inspiring. Rob's strength and tenacity shine through even in the most challenging of times. He effortlessly pulls the reader into his world and leaves them feeling full of hope and ready to overcome their own challenges head first."

—**LISA HARVEY-DUREN**, former founding executive director and board member of the Myotonic Dystrophy Foundation

"Life has a maddening tendency to toss a curveball at just the wrong time. No matter the problem or provocation, *Everest Strong* will guide you to the silver lining and beyond. Besecker's brilliant memoir is an inspired testament to the power of perseverance and a welcome reminder that redemption is always within reach."

—**JIM SKOGSBERGH**, president and CEO, Advocate Health Care

"I had the honor of meeting Rob Besecker in Nepal in 2015. We had something in common: a dream. He wanted to reach Everest Base Camp; me and my team, the Everest and Lhotse summits. After a couple of days, we, as a team, were convinced of something: Rob was a real hero. Any other person facing similar circumstances wouldn't be there. But he was. Reading this memoir, I am as inspired as I was the day I saw him arrive to the Base Camp—making his dream come true, one step at a time."

—**RODRIGO LARA-FERNANDEZ**, training and development consultant and mountaineer

"This is the kind of book the world needs today. We need good stories and real heroes. Here you have both: a great man facing a tremendous challenge, as a hero. What an inspirational story."

—**ERNESTO OLIVARES-MIRANDA**, speaker and mountaineer

"*Everest Strong* is Rob Besecker. Like being born with a genetic disease, climbing a mountain requires a special skill and strength to navigate the path. Advising Rob through his life as one of his doctors, I find his choices give us all hope and motivation. He knew I wasn't thrilled about his going up a mountain, but this book shows us how he did everything to coordinate and prepare expertly and convince us all of the importance of this mission while pursuing his goal."

—**ELIZABETH MCNALLY**, ward professor and director, Center for Genetic Medicine, Northwestern University

"*Everest Strong* is triumphant—a must-read! I was impressed and inspired by Rob Besecker's attitude and perspective. He shows all of us that it's not what life deals you but how you react, and the importance of following your heart. Everyone who reads this book will contemplate their heart, their strength, and how they live their life."

—**AUGIE NIETO**, chairman of ALS Therapy Development Institute, cofounder of Life Fitness and Augie's Quest to Cure ALS, and coauthor of *Augie's Quest: One Man's Journey from Success to Significance*

"Rob Besecker's strength and, even more impressive, his never-ending positive attitude, shine through in *Everest Strong*. He has endured so much yet continually displays remarkable courage and grace that inspires all who have the pleasure of knowing him. I have been touched by his patient advocacy and tireless desire to raise awareness. He is truly an awe-inspiring heart warrior."

—**HOLLY MORRELL**, founder and executive director,
Heartfelt Cardiac Projects

"This is a story of resilience, perseverance, perspective, mindset, and passion, and a shining example of the power of the human spirit to overcome overwhelming odds to live a rich, full life. If you want confidence and courage to take on your own challenges and live life full-out, no matter what life throws your way . . . you need to read *Everest Strong*!"

—**CHRISTINE SUVA**, founder and president of THRIVE Coach
Services, Inc. and coauthor of *Conscious Business Growth* and
The Change 7: Insights into Self-Empowerment

"*Everest Strong* is a highly inspirational true story offering enduring encouragement to readers, whatever challenges they face. The brave choices the author makes to embrace life when all odds are against him will uplift and remain with you."

—**TERRI SEVERIN**, speaker and author of *In the Wake of the Storm:
Living Beyond the Tragedy of Flight 4184*

"A mutual friend introduced me to 'an incredible guy you just have to meet' several years ago. I didn't know much regarding his health until I spoke with him. You would never know from looking at Rob the health challenges that have been put in front of him and his ability to conquer them. His strength and confidence show in his personality and his zest for life. *Everest Strong* is raw and real—just like Rob—and just like him, it shows us all that the sky is the limit."

—**KELLI MCDONALD**, MS Run the US relay runner

EVEREST STRONG

Dear Sir,

Stay Strong and always pursue
your goals and dreams!

[signature]

EVEREST STRONG

Reaching New Heights with Chronic Illness

An Inspirational Memoir

ROB BESECKER

Foreword by Steven M. Derks, former president and
CEO of the Muscular Dystrophy Association

Published 2017
Printed in the United States of America
Hardcover ISBN: 978-0-9994394-0-1
Paperback ISBN: 978-0-9994394-1-8
E-ISBN: 978-0-9994394-2-5
Library of Congress Control Number: 2017914897

Cover and interior design by Tabitha Lahr
Interior mountain icon © www.flaticon.com

For information, address: RobBesecker@EverestStrongRB.com

DISCLAIMER: There are as many versions of an individual's history as there are people included. This is mine. In order to protect the privacy of certain individuals and companies, I have changed some names, places and recognizable details mentioned in the book.

CONTENTS

PART III

FOREWORD

first had the pleasure of meeting Rob Besecker in July 2016. I was preparing for the Rock 'n' Roll Denver Half-Marathon that I would run in November as part of the Muscular Dystrophy Association (MDA) Team Momentum endurance running and fundraising program, and I had just finished a seven-mile group training run on the Chicago lakefront.

After the run on that hot, humid day, I was asked to thank the runners and say a few words.

I talked about the importance of MDA's recent rebrand—the connection it had to our endurance running program and how we were all "moving our muscles to help strengthen the muscles of people with muscular dystrophy and ALS." I told the group we worked hard to reflect the spirit of our families and those living with debilitating muscle disease. I recounted how, with the help of then-ninety-year-old Jerry Lewis, Natalie Morales from the *Today Show*, a number of other dignitaries, and, most important, our families, we had recently announced MDA's new branding—"*For Strength, Independence and Life*"—and our "*Live Unlimited*" campaign at Carnegie Hall in New York, the place where the first MDA Labor Day Telethon was hosted in 1966. Although we were all tired and very hot from the run, everyone seemed to listen attentively, and they applauded when I finished. I was pleased with myself.

Then our Chicago endurance program manager, April, called Rob Besecker up to the front of the group, and a handsome, fit, five-foot-eleven-inch man joined me where I stood.

"Good morning," Rob began. "After living with severe back injury and cardiac problems, including multiple surgeries and the implantation of a defibrillator/pacemaker for my heart in 2003, I was diagnosed with Myotonic Muscular Dystrophy (MMD) in 2006—a rare and degenerating neuromuscular disease. My father also had MMD. In 2012, after a particularly rough year, I set a goal to hike to Base Camp on Mount Everest at 17,600 feet of elevation. On April 20, 2015, after years of preparation and an eleven-day ascent, despite my health challenges and concerns expressed by my doctors, I made it! I am here today to say 'thank you' to you for running marathons and half marathons to raise awareness and funds for research, services, and support for people like me so we can go after our dreams and goals."

Cue the mouths dropping open, applause, and me slipping to the back of the crowd.

In sixty seconds, Rob became the personification of fighting for "strength, independence and life." And his presence and brief remarks that day did more to help our volunteers and runners understand MDA's mission and inspire their training than a CEO like me could ever hope to achieve.

As you will read in the following pages, Rob has endured and fought through many personal, family, and health setbacks and obstacles. In this book, he shares his approach, his thoughts, and his authentic emotions with readers—and in doing so, he reminds us of the importance of our life's journey and our remarkable opportunities to engage, learn, and grow.

Appropriately, at the beginning of Chapter 21, Rob quotes Sir Edmund Hillary (of Everest fame): "People don't decide to be extraordinary. They decide to accomplish extraordinary things." Rob has indeed accomplished an extraordinary thing in achieving his goal to get to Everest Base, but he is even more extraordinary for the way he chooses to live: unlimited.

Enjoy Rob's book . . . and carpe diem!

—Steven M. Derks
Former president and CEO
Muscular Dystrophy Association

INTRODUCTION

Have you ever given up on a goal because the people in your life said you couldn't do it, or woken up in the morning and not wanted to move because you felt completely overwhelmed—felt that you didn't have the tools (physical, mental, spiritual, or emotional) to succeed? We all face detours and obstacles in our lives that oftentimes feel insurmountable—whether it's the loss of a job, the death of a loved one, the end of a relationship, the fear of the unknown, or a major health battle.

In 2000, at the age of twenty-five, I was diagnosed with heart disease. In 2003, due to additional cardiac abnormalities, I underwent my first cardiac surgery to install a pacemaker/defibrillator to assist with my ailing heart. From there, my physical health and emotional well-being continued to deteriorate, and there was a great deal of uncertainty as to how my growing health issues would impact my future.

As I battled my demons and fought back from additional heart disease and surgeries, including five cardiac procedures in 2011, the mental anguish nearly drove me to a state of depression. Many physicians and friends began questioning whether I would survive and doubting my resilience. Upon my recovery, other patients and clinicians asked me how I was able to stay so positive and keep going.

But what other option did I have?

As I see it, we only have two options when things don't go our way: we can either dwell on the negative until it consumes us, or—though it is extremely difficult to do when it feels like the world is plotting against us—we can focus on the positive and find ways to overcome and adapt to the situation. Simply put, we can give up and quit, or we can move forward and make the best of a less-than-ideal circumstance, take control of our own fate, and not leave our future to chance.

For me, giving up was never an acceptable outcome. Instead, I stood up against the critics who felt I couldn't push forward and turned my attention to the supporters who fueled my energy to proceed. Through many different ups and downs, various trials and tribulations, and some good ole common sense, I found a path that worked for me. It's a path I have also seen work for others, and it operates on a common-sense principle: we must put our energy into something productive rather than spinning our wheels on the alternative.

In 2012, I began my tedious recovery and set my sights on a lofty goal that none of my physicians thought I could achieve. I sought to put an exclamation point on my recovery; and what better way to renew my independence than by trekking to the tallest mountain in the world? In spite of all the challenges I endured, it was the most difficult thing I ever tried to do—on purpose—and it took every ounce of strength and courage I had.

What does "being strong" mean? We each have our own definition. I used to think it was strictly a physical description referring to a power or supremacy over an object or individual, and that sensitivity equated to weakness. Through the years, I've learned that "being strong" can also include the ability to focus through and withstand a heavy burden, that being emotionally honest and vulnerable builds character. Strength isn't about comparing our situation to others or manipulating something out of our control. It is taking the opportunity to manage our lives, to not be complacent in despair but to pursue goals and dreams. The simple fact that I reached for that mountain—that I tried and gave it my best effort—meant that I had become "Everest Strong." Whether I ultimately overcame the mountain or not was irrelevant.

We are all unique, and we each have different wants and desires to shoot for. Whatever your aspirations may be and whatever challenges you are facing, I hope this book inspires you to rise above those obstacles and not be afraid of trying, and to come out on the other side a stronger, better version of yourself. By never giving up and always working toward your goals and dreams, you too can become "strong."

PROLOGUE

March 13, 2011, 2:30 a.m.

> *911, What is your emergency?*
> *My defibrillator went off twice.*
> *What's your name, sir?*
> *Robert Besecker.*
> *Where are you?*
> *I'm home.*
> *Is anyone there with you?*
> *No, I'm alone.*
> *Is your front door open?*
> *No, it's locked.*
> *Sir, if you can, please unlock your door so the paramedics*
> *will be able to easily enter your house.*
> *(brief silence)*
> *I'll try . . .*

Just a few days earlier, I had been released from the hospital after a procedure that was supposed to heal my ailing heart. Now here I was, calling 911 to be sent back.

I was thirty-seven years old and had suffered from chronic and progressive heart ailments and muscular dystrophy for many years. My physicians had recommended a cardiac ablation for atrial fibrillation, an increasingly common procedure to correct irregular heartbeats. I'd been a bit skeptical about the procedure when my doctor first made the suggestion more than a year earlier, but as time went by and I could feel the rhythm of my heart worsening and becoming increasingly erratic and uncomfortable, it became clear I would need to have the surgery, like it or not.

There were just some scheduling conflicts to figure out.

First, I had made arrangements to run the Chicago Hot Chocolate 5K in November. I didn't want to miss that after completing my first-ever 5K earlier that year.

Second, I'd planned a trip to Antarctica, my seventh and final continent to visit, for December. If I had surgery beforehand, I might be in the midst of my recovery and unable to go.

My heart would just have to hold on.

And it did. I ran the 5K and traveled to Antarctica and back just in time for my ablation, a procedure in which a thin wire that sends electrical impulses is guided into the heart and used to destroy small areas of tissue that are causing a rapid or irregular heart rhythm.

The surgery that Wednesday went beautifully, my physicians assured me afterward, which was both expected and uncomforting at the same time. From my perspective, the experience had been hellish, a series of procedures that included having a hose put down my throat, tubes inserted in my arms, and catheters thrust up my groin and shoved into my heart, followed by six hours of forced immobility—the last part being the most emotionally exhausting and physically uncomfortable.

My doctors released me the following day, assuring me I could return to work on Monday, just as long as I took it easy over the weekend.

"No problem," I said, grinning. "I love watching TV!"

They smiled, thinking I was joking. By that time, they were accustomed to my activity levels and love of travel. But it was true. I love movies and TV shows, and I fully intended to take advantage of the days ahead by resting and relaxing and catching up on some much-needed down time.

Despite having followed doctor's orders since leaving the hospital three days earlier, however, as I headed down the hall to go to bed at 2:30 a.m. that Sunday morning, I began to feel a terrible discomfort. When

I stopped in the bathroom, I nearly fell over. Suddenly, the discomfort became much worse and I felt my heart racing faster than ever.

I scrambled to my bed to lie down, trying to relax and stay calm. My house was pitch-black except for a small lamp next to my bed. Then suddenly, *WHAM!!!* My defibrillator fired.

Some people describe the feeling of a defibrillator firing like being kicked in the chest by a horse or struck by lightning, but I would liken the sensation to the shock of touching an electric fence multiplied by a factor of one hundred. It was the worst experience I've ever endured. Though the defibrillator makes no sound and the physical pain lasts only a fraction of a second, it was so violent it made me sit straight up in my bed in absolute shock, petrified.

I took some deep breaths and recalled my physician's directions. He had said that I would know immediately if my device went off, and boy was he right. He also told me that if it went off only once I shouldn't worry; I should just call him the next business day and let him know. All I had to do was lie down and relax.

How in the world anyone could relax after a chest blow like that baffled me, but I tried to do just that. I lay back down.

WHAM!!! It went off again, every bit as violently as the first time.

"If your device goes off twice," I recalled him saying, "call 911."

The moment I set the phone down after the 911 call, *WHAM!!!*—the defibrillator went off *again*. I was frozen with fear; I didn't want to move. But the words of the dispatcher resonated in my head. I had to make it to my front door and unlock it so the paramedics could reach me.

Focus, Rob, I told myself. *Stay focused. Get to the door.*

The door seemed so very far away.

That's okay, just get out of bed and reach the light switch in the hall. Just take a few steps to the hallway and turn on the light. Then you can make it to the door. One step at a time.

I hurried to the switch, eager to flood the hallway with light and erase the darkness threatening to take my life.

WHAM!!! This time, the violence of the shock brought me to my knees. I tried to rise again, but the tightness in my chest held me down.

Get to the door, Rob, get to the door.

I'd competed in so many athletic events, traveled to so many places, and reached so many goals. This, my simplest goal ever—*reach the front door*—was proving to be one of the most insurmountable.

If I didn't unlock the door, the two alternatives were dying or *having to replace the damn door.* Images rushed through my head of the police and paramedics kicking down my door, taking me away to the hospital, and leaving my home open to the world. I had to reach the front door.

As I crawled forward on my forearms and knees, my heart rate went through the roof, beating as if a machine gun, not a defibrillator, was firing deep into my chest.

When I finally reached the door and opened it, a blast of noise screamed through the night.

Damn! I forgot to turn off the alarm.

I let it scream. I didn't have the strength to stand, much less punch in the code, so I lay sprawled out on the hallway floor while my defibrillator went off another three times.

I had absolutely no idea what was going on but I knew one thing: lying on the floor waiting to die was not an option. So I crawled a little bit farther, struggling for every inch, until I reached my living room recliner, which I managed to climb into. And there I remained—motionless, cold, terrified, exhausted, and waiting for help.

In the five minutes I lay there with the alarm still screaming, the failings of my life played before me.

Life will go on without you, an abstract voice taunted me.

I moved my head from left to right as if trying to shake off the voice. Like the alarm, it wouldn't be silenced.

You've never been married, it scolded me.

"Shut up!" I hissed through my teeth.

You've never had children, it retaliated.

Tears slowly slid down my cheeks. Whatever that voice was, it knew me well. It knew my weaknesses, my longings, and my fears. Soon, my own thoughts began to mimic the voice.

What if I never have a wife to grow old with? What if I never have kids to take to a baseball game? What if I never grow old?

The bright lights of the ambulance arriving burst through the front window, shaking me out of that state of mind and bringing me back to my living room. A police officer was the first to enter. He assessed the situation and silenced the alarm; the paramedics followed soon after and began asking me questions and taking my vitals.

For a brief moment, I felt secure, like I could relax and take a deep breath. I was no longer completely alone; help had arrived. I'd been rescued.

Then, just when I thought I was safe—*WHAM!!!* The paramedics scrambled to figure out what was happening. Was the problem with my heart or a defect with my defibrillator?

My device fired a total of eighteen times that night, half of which occurred with the paramedics by my side as I lay helpless on my living room recliner. Each shock was every bit as painful and even more horrific than the last. At times, I belted out a brief scream in response to the blows. The anticipation of another impending jolt was terrifying.

Blood wasn't circulating properly through my body, and my hands and feet felt like ice blocks. I was freezing cold and shivering yet drenched in sweat from my heart racing and chest pounding.

"What is his heart rate?" one paramedic asked the other.

"I don't know," he answered, "but it's way too fast."

They wasted no more time. I was strapped to a stretcher and hurried into an ambulance; the serious looks on the paramedics' faces did nothing to calm me.

On our way to the hospital, I looked up at the paramedic squatting beside me and, in the calmest voice I could manage, I asked her, "Am I going to die?"

She looked at me with an intense stare, as if trying to find a way to reassure me while still telling me the truth. She then looked down, took a deep breath, and turned her eyes back to me. "Not if I can help it," she replied, almost as if to herself.

I nodded, grateful to have her on my side.

I was so very tired, but terrified of falling asleep. I kept thinking of how in the movies when someone is dying, another person hovers above them and says, "Hang on, don't close your eyes!" I desperately wanted to close my eyes, to let my mind and body rest.

Instead, I talked. I answered what seemed like a million questions from the paramedic while en route to the hospital. I talked to stay alive.

I had no idea as I lay shivering on that cold March night, wondering if I would live or die, that this was the first night of the rest of my life—that this night would be what challenged me to climb Mount Everest.

Still, nothing could have prepared me for the calamity that hit once I was up in the Himalayan mountains—or the tragedy that struck after I'd hiked back down.

PART I

CHAPTER 1

GROWING PAINS

I don't want expensive gifts; I don't want to be bought. I have
everything I want. I just want someone to be there for me, to
make me feel safe and secure.
                                                    —Princess Diana

I hardly had the "Disney" version of childhood growing up in a south-west suburb of Chicago. While "dysfunctional" may be an overused term these days, when it comes to my family, it really is the best way to describe our dynamic.

My dad was a well-educated man yet rough and tough—the kind of guy who would grin and bear it and never reveal his softer side. My mom, on the other hand, was kind and thoughtful, and tried to be a devoted mother, but was plagued by alcoholism and depression that at times led to suicidal tendencies.

The two of them fought constantly—just like my three older siblings and I did. Cindy, who was six years older than me, picked on me as a kid and pushed me around, locking me in closets if I didn't follow her direction. My brother Rusty, who was eight years older, became violent and unpredictable after being diagnosed with paranoid schizophrenia and turning to drugs and alcohol. My oldest sister, Chris, who is fourteen years older than I am, left the house as soon as she could to escape the family and started dating Pat, the man she'd eventually marry (and later divorce) and who became like another big brother to me.

Despite the conflicts of growing up in a noisy household with four kids, two dogs, and two cats led by battling parents, our home was filled with as much humor and pride as drama and rage.

With little confidence as a result of my home life, I found myself an easy target at school. I've always had a lazy eye, and back then I wore an eye patch to help correct my vision. The older kids called me Captain Hook and often ganged up on me, pushing me until I tripped and fell.

Eventually I discovered I could make people laugh, and that made life easier. I became the class clown at school and at home, doing my best to make any tense situation a little more bearable.

To escape the volatility of my family life and bullying at school, I also threw myself into sports. They became my world, my refuge. I was involved in just about any sport imaginable—baseball, basketball, football—anything that could keep me out of the house. I excelled at every one of them.

That was partly due to my father's influence. He was constantly pushing me to succeed—and pushing hard.

There is one game I especially remember. I was about ten years old and playing in a Hickory Hills youth baseball all-star tournament. It was the top of the last inning; my team was down by a run, and I was leading off. I stood at the plate, the bat heavy in my hands, knowing my teammates and fans were counting on me and it was up to me to get things started. If I didn't, we'd lose the game.

Then came the ball.

Whack! I hit the ball and watched it fly in an ineffective arc over the infield before falling straight back down into the pitcher's glove about fifteen feet in front of me. I'd hit a pop-out that would cost us the game—and eliminate us from the tournament.

I had failed. I felt awful and ashamed.

After every game, win or lose, my team always got pizza from the concession stand. But my dad wasn't going to let that happen today.

"You're not getting any damned pizza," he said, dragging me off to the car as my mother scurried behind. "You lost the game. You suck at baseball. We're going home."

I cried all the way home but he wouldn't let up.

"You're fucking useless!" he screamed, giving me holy hell.

"Russell, stop it!" my mother said.

My dad brushed her off as if she was talking to herself and just kept at it.

By the time we got home I was nothing but tears, and all I wanted to do was run to my room and throw myself on the bed.

"Go cry in your room!" my dad snapped. "You make me sick!"

Half an hour later, I heard the phone ringing downstairs. A couple of minutes later, my mother was standing in my doorway, a show of concern on her face.

"Robby, they need you back at the tournament. Hurry up and get your uniform back on!"

"What do you mean?" I asked, still blubbering and completely confused.

"The boy who pitched the final inning had already pitched more innings than he was allowed. You have to go back and replay the last inning!"

My mom was happy to see we had another chance to win the game, but to me, playing the inning over felt like one more chance to fail; I didn't want to go. Yet there was a feeling inside me that said I needed to get back out there.

Later in life, I would grow to realize that this feeling would always be there in times of adversity, encouraging me to get up and keep going no matter how grim the situation. The pressure would be converted to energy, and disappointment would become opportunity. On this particular day, however, I only felt a glimmer of that possibility.

During the entire drive back to the ballpark, my father clenched the steering wheel, yelling at me. "You'd better not fuck this up again! Don't be a loser this time."

My mom continued to grumble, but she knew she was powerless

against his anger. He was going to say what he wanted to say—namely, that I was nothing but a disappointment.

When it was my turn to lead off the top of the seventh inning again, I went up to bat and fouled the very first pitch out of play, all the way down the right field line. The coach from the other team began screaming to his players, "Move over, move over! He's going to hit the ball to right field."

I stood there listening to the other team jeer, knowing my dad was watching me. Then another pitch came.

I swung with all my might and tore the cover off that damned ball. I let it rip clear over the left field fence, hitting a home run that made our team go wild. I circled the bases as my teammates and fans roared.

We ended up coming back and winning the game!

When it was over, my teammates pounded me on the back, screaming with joy, but I just felt numb, the barrage of insults from my father still fresh in my mind.

My dad came over and stood a short distance from me. I glanced up at him and back down.

"Come here," he said, gesturing with his head.

"No," I said, looking down at my shoes.

"I said, get over here. Now!"

I got up and slowly walked toward him, my head still hanging low.

When I reached him, he put his arm around me and gave me a firm hug and a kiss on the cheek. "I love you," he told me.

It was the first time I'd heard him say that to me, as far as I could remember.

Though he didn't say those words to me again until he was on his deathbed, I came to realize my father loved me very much. Because of how he was raised, he was rough around the edges at times, but there were softer emotions underneath his hard exterior.

I learned a valuable lesson that day, one that has helped me battle other challenges in my life: never give up. No matter how many times I got knocked down in life, I had to get back up. Despite the strange way my dad showed his affection, I knew it was out of love that he pushed me hard. And whenever I face a struggle today, there's my dad's voice inside of me, yelling for me to never quit—to get back up and fight no matter what the circumstance.

My dad acquired that strong sense of determination, will, and work ethic from his own father. My paternal grandpa was a successful, hard-working businessman who made a good living from a glass company he purchased and built up. He was someone I adored and looked up to.

"Robby," my grandpa said to me one day, "I want you to make me a promise."

"Sure, Grandpa," I said. "What is it?"

"I want you to promise me you'll never smoke cigarettes, drink alcohol, or chew tobacco until you're twenty-one. Will you promise me that?"

My grandpa wanted to make sure I didn't make the same mistakes as everyone else in my family. Both my parents had drinking problems, my brother had drinking and drug problems, and everyone in my family smoked.

I didn't think twice about it. "Yes, Grandpa," I said. "I promise."

We even signed a contract, with my father as a witness, to make our deal official.

My grandpa died in 1987, before I reached my twenty-first birthday, but that deal meant the world to me and became sacred for me. The act of making a promise put my honor on the line. I felt like keeping my word was the most valuable thing I could offer, especially in my family, which was so full of tension and mistrust. I decided I wasn't going to break that promise, no matter what—and I didn't.

Adhering to that agreement kept me somewhat isolated at times, since it meant avoiding many of the after-game parties with the guys on the football team, but I kept my word. Over time, I learned that was the most important thing.

As a result of my scholastic and athletic achievements, many colleges contacted me to play football for them; by the end of my junior year of high school the mailbox was regularly packed with thick manila envelopes from schools across the nation. I soon narrowed my options down to two: Arizona State University in Tempe and Northwestern University in Chicago.

The excitement and anticipation of playing college football came to a sudden halt, however, when I found out I had fractured vertebrae in my spine.

It wasn't one of those injuries that just happens suddenly, where one minute you're fine and the next there's a crack and you get carried away on a stretcher. It happened gradually. I tweaked my back one day during football drills, and it hurt like hell, but I continued to play through the soreness. Eventually, though, it got to a point where it was really swollen and I could barely stand up straight.

"You need to get to a doctor," my sister said when she stopped by the house and noticed me lying on an ice pack in substantial pain. Chris was a nurse and knew something was wrong.

X-rays of my back showed nothing, but when an orthopedist did a CT scan of my back, it told a different story.

"I'm afraid you've sustained a fracture in your fourth and fifth lower lumbar vertebrae," he said. "An injury like this can quickly degenerate and you could find yourself facing chronic back pain for the rest of your life. I can't clear you to play football with an injury like this."

With that devastating news, my football career was over. I quickly went from rising football star to a has-been that never really was. The scholarships went away, and I was unable to play my senior year.

Coincidentally, my father once had a similar experience. He was a big football star in high school who won a full scholarship to Purdue University, but he tore a ligament in his knee the first week of practice his freshman year. After a year of rehabilitation, he broke his ankle the first day back to practice his sophomore year. After that, he never played football again.

Fortunately, after going through a rigorous off-season training program to rehabilitate my back, I recuperated enough to play baseball. I put all my energies into excelling during that final season of high school ball, and the hard work paid off: I was voted All-Conference my senior year.

That summer, I applied to the Illinois Institute of Technology, where I was offered a baseball scholarship. I was also selected to play on Team Chicago, an all-star traveling team that would play against the junior national teams in Germany and Amsterdam. Shortly after my eighteenth birthday, I left the country for the first time.

I was thrilled to be part of Team Chicago—but misfortune soon struck again. A week into our trip, while we were in Germany, I had to be rushed to the hospital after a bad fall. I landed on some broken glass and sliced my hand all the way down to the bone, soaking my clothes with gushing blood. I couldn't play baseball for the remainder of the trip and was forced to support my team from the bench while wearing a cast.

While I was devastated by another restrictive injury, the positive of the trip was that it awakened my desire to travel and see the world. I wasn't a fullback or linebacker anymore, but I was coming to realize that there was an entire world before me, and I had the strength and stamina to explore it. I didn't need to use force and ram my way through every obstacle; I could plan for and reason my way around the roadblocks I encountered. It occurred to me that my physical struggles and involvement in athletics had taught me a lot more than how to play ball and take a hit; they had educated me on the importance of relationships, hard work, and focus. There was no adventure I couldn't pursue, I reasoned, if I made it a goal.

During college, I enjoyed annual baseball trips to Florida, a summer jaunt to the Grand Canyon, and spring breaks to Lake Havasu and South Padre Island with friends. After graduation, I visited Washington, DC, went to Atlanta for the Olympics (an event made all the more memorable when a bomb went off in the very section I'd sat in the day after I was there), and went bungee jumping and skydiving.

I had majored in business with a focus in marketing and management at IIT, and I ultimately secured a management position with a major airline; in the years that followed, I took advantage of the cheap air travel I got through the company whenever I had time off. I traveled to Germany and Rome, to Cancun and Hawaii. I even ventured to Australia for a Shania Twain concert before the 2000 Summer Olympics after developing a friendship with a member of her band. When I returned from Australia, I realized I'd already been to three different continents and decided in that moment to make it a goal to see them all.

Closer to home, I took trips to Niagara Falls, Mount Rushmore, and Yellowstone National Park. I began to follow the Cubs on road trips to California, New York, and Texas. It wasn't long before I realized that, without even trying, I'd been to half the Major League Baseball stadiums in the country. With the ability to travel for next to nothing, I figured, *Why not see them all?* (Years later, on August 6, 2014, I completed this goal at Safeco Field in Seattle.)

I was twenty-five, strong, energetic, successful, and having the time of my life. But in the spring of 2000, all of that would change . . .

CHAPTER 2:

THERE GOES MY HEART

An object in motion tends to remain in motion along a straight line unless acted upon by an outside force.

—Isaac Newton

My life as I knew it all began to unravel one evening in March 2000. My parents were home, my aunt and uncle were visiting from Florida, and my sisters, Chris and Cindy, had come over. We were all having a nice family night, sitting around the fireplace, watching TV, and talking, when my heart began to race uncontrollably. It went from a normal rhythm to a rapid thumping in a matter of seconds—like I'd just gone from lounging in a cabana to sprinting the 100-meter dash in the midst of a hot sauna.

I was sweating profusely and it was really uncomfortable. I'd had a similar sensation while visiting Paris the summer before, but had dismissed it given the abundance of food I'd been eating. This time, however, it was impossible to ignore.

I looked over at Chris, who had worked in trauma units and the emergency room.

"Hey, Chris," I said through the chatter of family conversation and television noise in the background. "Can you check my heart rate?"

"Why?" she asked. "What's wrong?"

"Nothing," I said, thinking it would be something insignificant.

Chris took my wrist and checked my pulse. "Holy shit, Robby!" she said. "How long has this been happening? Did it just start?"

"I don't know," I said, now nervous. "Maybe fifteen minutes?"

"Your pulse is irregular and way too fast," Chris said, already walking to the phone. She called the hospital where she worked, and the doctor she spoke to told her to bring me to the hospital right away.

Before I knew it, I was in the ER, hooked up to a matrix of electronic cords and machines. At one point, my heart rate soared above 250 beats per minute—which, given that a normal resting heart rate is usually between sixty and one hundred beats per minute, and as low as forty for an athlete, is far faster than any heart should beat. For someone of my age and fitness level, my heart was beating three to four times faster than it should have been. Something was seriously wrong.

Heart problems were nothing new in my family. My mother's brother had died of a sudden cardiac death when he was only sixteen years old, and my mother and another of her brothers both had pacemakers. My father's side of the family wasn't much better: his brother had died from a heart attack during an epileptic seizure and various uncles had died from heart attacks. The realization that I might have inherited these genetic traits hit me hard. Was I going to drop dead at a young age like my mother's brother?

I spent three days in the hospital under observation before the doctors told me I had atrial fibrillation, an irregular heartbeat that can cut blood flow and lead to heart failure, strokes, and other serious complications. It was the same disorder my mother and her brother had.

A normal and healthy heart beats regularly, like the rhythm of a steady military march going *left . . . left . . . left, right, left.* My atrial fibrillation, or AFib as it's commonly called, made it so I would experience very unpleasant arrhythmias, as if some soldiers in the march were walking, others were jogging, and even more were running, causing the entire group to become out of whack.

AFib affects about three percent of the population and most often occurs in mid to late life; it is rarely seen in young people. Yet here I was, a twenty-six-year-old athlete who rarely drank alcohol and had never smoked or used drugs, and I had the heart of an old man!

"I wouldn't worry," the doctor said. "AFib is often episodic and simply goes away. Let's just keep an eye on it and, hopefully, you won't have any more problems."

He told me to get plenty of rest and to begin a consistent exercise program in combination with a healthy and more balanced diet. He also gave me some beta blockers to take in order to suppress the abnormal heart rhythms. Though I rarely drank alcohol and the doctor felt it was unrelated, I decided to stop consuming alcohol altogether.

Other than that, there was no solution, no game plan. I had a rare heart condition for someone my age but was told not to worry. It might get better or it might not. That was it. As for any further episodes of AFib? I was simply instructed to take an extra dose of the beta blocker and try to relax whenever they occurred.

By May, I was accepted into the MBA program at Purdue University—where my father had also earned his bachelor's and master's degrees. So I moved to Lafayette, Indiana, and hunkered down for grad school.

As for my health? My biggest concerns were the side effects of the beta blockers I began taking after the AFib diagnosis—namely, the dizzy spells I experienced if I stood up too quickly, which made me feel like I was going to faint. The feeling passed quickly, however, and I learned to take my time getting up from a seated position. All in all, I saw it as a minor inconvenience, and one I could live with.

▲▲ ▲▲ ▲▲

After graduating in 2002, I accepted a management-track rotational position in human resources with an amazing technology company in Hartford, Connecticut. I was now in the aerospace and defense industry, a sector I long had wanted to work in. I had always been very patriotic and had considered joining the military after high school. I worked hard, maybe harder than I'd ever worked before, at this new job, and the hard work paid off as I continued to move forward with the company.

I also loved living in Connecticut—meeting new people, playing softball and indoor soccer, and hanging out with friends several nights a week.

Life was good, really good—until everything fell apart.

It was St. Patrick's Day, 2003. I was meeting with a recruiter from the Army at the Wood-N-Tap Bar and Grill. She was a friend of a friend and we were meeting to discuss the possibility of my joining the Army Reserve. I knew my heart would be an issue, but I was optimistic there would be some way to work around it since I was in such good shape and my conditions weren't noticeable.

We barely had time to order our appetizers and drinks before President George Bush appeared on the small TV perched high in the corner of the bar. The bar patrons fell silent as President Bush described the increasingly tense state of the world in the two years following 9/11, the rising aggressions in the Middle East, and the growing threat to world peace and American security. Then he warned of what was coming.

"All the decades of deceit and cruelty have now reached an end," he declared. "Saddam Hussein and his sons must leave Iraq within forty-eight hours. Their refusal to do so will result in military conflict commenced at a time of our choosing."

The recruiter and I looked at each other as the realization sunk in: America was going to war.

All I've ever wanted is to lead a heroic life. I have never been one to retreat when things get rough—probably an outcome of growing up in a family so scarred by damage, conflict, and tough love. If I could save someone, I would. If I could give my life so another could live, I would. I wanted to do something valuable with my life. There was no way to justify staying home and watching movies when I could be defending our nation with my fellow Americans in the Middle East.

Still shaken by the president's words, I came to the harsh realization that I might be deployed overseas if I joined the Army Reserve.

First, though, I had to get medical clearance.

A few weeks later, I was in the office of my new primary care physician, Dr. Frances Gurtman, explaining to her my interest in getting off the beta blockers and, more important, finding a cardiologist. If I could meet with a cardiologist, I reasoned, he or she could confirm that my heart was fine. It might have an occasional irregularity but it was hardly incapacitating.

"I think that's a reasonable course of action," she said, looking over my medical records. "If you want to stop taking the beta blockers and there aren't any further incidents—and if your cardiologist supports that decision—I have no problem with it."

After receiving a recommendation and referral for a local cardiologist, I thanked her and left the office, confident that I was already halfway to joining the military and defending our nation. I couldn't have been more thrilled.

I arranged an appointment with a young cardiologist, Dr. Melissa Ferraro, who had already established an impressive reputation in cardiovascular disease and other heart conditions. I was impressed with her immediately. Not only did she see me for my first appointment within days, she also reviewed my medical charts ahead of time and listened attentively as I nonchalantly listed my family history of heart problems, along with my own experiences. As far as I was concerned, my heart had a minor abnormality that could easily be dealt with, and the dizzy spells I'd had since starting to take the beta blockers were my biggest problem.

"So, really what I'm asking is, can I stop taking the heart medication and join the military?" I said. "I've been taking these beta blockers for three years and there's been no change in my symptoms, and I feel fine."

"Well," she said, nodding agreeably, "I'd like to check into it further to be sure that everything is okay before I say yes to anything. So why don't we run a couple of tests, and if everything checks out, then we can discuss it further. How's that sound?"

"Sounds good!" I said.

I left her office feeling like I was on top of the world. A few routine tests and I'd be cleared and ready to move forward! Finally, I felt like I was heading somewhere special with my life.

"Do you have a few minutes?" I asked cheerfully as I walked into my boss's office to inform him about my upcoming tests.

"Sure, Rob, sit down. What's up?" he asked, leaning back in his chair.

We'd developed a good relationship, and I was comfortable talking to him. "It's nothing, really," I began. "I'm just being checked for some heart conditions and I'm hoping we can be somewhat flexible with my work schedule to set the appointments. I'll stay on top of everything and won't fall behind. I just have to go in for these tests over the next week."

As he lowered his eyes and leaned forward, the look of concern on his face was unmistakable. "Heart conditions? Is everything okay? It isn't anything serious, I hope."

"Oh, no, no. It's just some basic stuff I need to get checked out, nothing major."

"Of course, Rob," he said. "Take whatever time you need and take care of yourself. Do what you need to do and let me know if there's anything I can do to help." He smiled.

With that I was out the door and on my way to my next appointment with Dr. Ferraro.

▲▲ ▲▲ ▲▲

"All right, Rob," Dr. Ferraro said, holding a tape recorder–sized device with an array of cords. "I want you to wear this for the weekend so we can see what's going on with your heart. Any time you start to feel anything unusual—any palpitations, dizzy spells, anything at all—I want you to press this button. That will give us a marker, and we'll be able to see what was going on with your heart at that precise moment."

She handed me the device, which she said was called a cardiac event recorder, and showed me how to wear it, sticking the combination of electrodes at strategic points on my chest and then tucking the recorder in my pocket.

The instructions were simple: press the button when a dizzy spell came on and the device would record my heart rhythm for five minutes, including the moments before I hit the button.

To add to the bizarre nature of the test, I was heading to Chicago that weekend and had to board a plane while wearing this electronic device strapped to my chest. I'd have to leave for the airport even earlier than usual, as I would have some explaining to do with airport security.

The entire experience was rather uncomfortable. Removing the stickers daily before I showered and replacing them afterward became a pain. The process irritated my skin, making it itchy. However, it was pretty amazing that my every heartbeat could be measured at the push of a button.

I'd worn a similar type of device a few times in the past, something called a Holter monitor that recorded my heart's activity continuously. That one had been a pain because it hindered so many of my routine activities, like showering or dressing. At least this one was far less intrusive— or maybe I was just getting used to such things.

On the flight back from Chicago to Hartford, I found myself sitting in a middle seat. I'd asked the flight attendant if there was any chance of my moving, explaining to her that I was laced up with heart monitoring equipment, but she told me the flight was full and there was nothing she could do.

Shortly before takeoff, a woman in an aisle seat a few rows in front of me started raising hell and was taken off the plane. It worked in my favor.

"Sir," the same flight attendant came back to ask, "would you like to move to that aisle seat?"

"Thank you so much," I replied. "I'd be happy to." As I stood up, bending my head under the overhead luggage compartment, a dizzy spell hit.

This is it, I thought, hitting the button on my monitor as I'd been instructed. Finally, Dr. Ferraro would be able to see what was happening during the annoying dizzy spells I'd told her about.

After a few seconds, the feeling went away. I grabbed my carry-on and moved to the new aisle seat, where I stretched my legs out in luxurious comfort.

▲▲ ▲▲ ▲▲

A few days later, I was at my usual Wednesday night softball game, which was just about ready to begin, when my cell phone rang. It was Dr. Ferraro.

"Hey, doc, what's up?" I asked her.

"I'm afraid it's not good, Rob," she said.

"What do you mean?"

"Do you remember the event you had this past weekend?" Her voice was somber, and I knew whatever it was, it was serious.

"Sure," I said, "I had another one of those dizzy spells while I was on the plane flying back to Connecticut. That's what I've been telling you about. What's wrong?"

"When you were feeling that dizzy spell, your heart stopped. It stopped beating."

Stopped beating? How could my heart stop beating? I was stunned. "What do you mean?" I asked, thinking, *That's crazy.*

"Your heart stopped pumping blood for four seconds. There's something seriously wrong. We need to get these tests underway as soon as possible so we can figure out what's going on."

As Dr. Ferraro talked, I just stood there, feeling my heartbeat—thump, thump, thump. It felt as normal as ever.

"I don't want you playing any sports. No softball, no jogging, and I don't want you driving until we figure this out. This is not something to mess around with. Do you understand?"

Given the fact that I felt fine and was already at the softball field, I wasn't inclined to sit the game out. So I told her I would play that night, then drive home and take it easy until we scheduled our next appointment. She wasn't happy with my decision, but she must have recognized my stubbornness, because she conceded after some back and forth.

I knew I had to be honest with my physicians. Concealing information wasn't going to help me get any better, and it could mean the difference between treatment that worked and treatment that didn't. Still, it really bothered me that my doctor didn't want me to play sports. And after I hung up, my mind was flooded with questions. How had my heart stopped beating and I didn't even know it? Were all those other dizzy spells the same thing? Was my heart just stopping and starting of its own accord? I couldn't comprehend it.

Since childhood, I'd trained myself to conceal my emotions, so instead of wallowing in the news, I toughened up and played softball. I didn't tell anyone about the phone call, or that I had any heart problem at all. I just played the game as if I were as fit as anyone else.

Playing sports was a big part of my world, and unless I needed to be rushed directly to the hospital, I was going to live my life. It was a small act of rebellion, but somehow, I needed that rebellion. I needed to feel I had some control, because everything was coming to feel so utterly, completely *out* of control.

▲▲ ▲▲ ▲▲

The following Monday, I had a full day of doctor's appointments. After getting a blood test on the third floor of the medical office building, I ran up the stairs to the eighth floor for an echocardiogram in Dr. Ferraro's office. By the time I got there, my heart was palpitating. I felt like a middle-aged guy who hadn't exercised in a decade.

During the entire test, my heart continued to palpitate.

"Can you feel that?" the cardiac technician asked, referring to my abnormal heart rhythm.

"Yes," I admitted.

When I met with Dr. Ferraro after the echocardiogram, she dropped another bomb on me.

"Have you ever heard of Noonan syndrome?" she asked.

"No," I said, shaking my head. "What's that?"

"I've been doing some research, and I think there's a possibility that some of your heart problems could be related to a congenital disorder called Noonan syndrome."

I had no idea what it was, but she certainly had my attention.

"We don't know a lot about it, and the diagnosis is difficult. We look for clusters of signs and symptoms, but basically it's characterized by a whole range of features. Congenital heart defects are almost always present, and other signs may include a thick-webbed neck, low hairline at the back of the neck, low-set ears with thick outer rims, visual problems, widely spaced and low-set nipples, intestinal abnormalities, and often learning disabilities."

I gave it some thought. As a baby I'd had a double hernia—an intestinal abnormality. Then I'd had a lazy eye and worn a patch as a kid. My family had often teased me and kids had bullied me at school and called me "no neck" because my neck was so short and thick. My ears? Yes, they were sort of low and really thick. My hairline also went very low on the back of my neck. All these things had never seemed like anything more than minor imperfections. Aside from the double hernia and heart problems, they'd seemed trivial. But now a doctor was telling me I might have a congenital syndrome that put all these pieces together. It was unbelievable.

"I'd like to send you to a geneticist," she said. "Dr. Greenstein at the University of Connecticut Hospital might be able to determine if you do have Noonan syndrome or not."

She wasted no time in getting me an appointment.

▲ ▲ ▲

Dr. Greenstein was a friendly, pleasant man. He listened in a way that many physicians don't. At first uncomfortable, I slowly relaxed, confident that I had found a physician who, like Dr. Ferraro, would pay attention not just to what was going on with my body but also with my emotional state.

He began the visit by taking some photos of me, getting shots of my neck, ears, chest, and so on. Then he drew up a family tree as I displayed photos of my relatives, which he'd asked me to bring ahead of time. We stopped at each family member to identify any health problems or unusual features. As we did, I began to realize that there were a number of oddities surrounding my family's health, including things like sudden cardiac death, heart rhythm abnormalities, short stature, big ears—the list went on. Nothing had seemed like a big deal to me before, but once I saw all the doctor's marks on my family tree, all those little things added up to one big thing: there seemed to be a congenital abnormality in my family.

Dr. Greenstein was especially interested in my uncle John, my mom's younger brother. John had died suddenly in gym class at the age of sixteen, back in 1954. I'd never noticed it before, but now that I'd learned about Noonan syndrome, I could tell my uncle John had many of the features: a short stature, awkward facial characteristics, and low-cupped ears.

"It does look like there's a good chance you have it too," Dr. Greenstein told me.

"And if I do have it," I said, "what are the chances of my children getting it?"

"About fifty-fifty," he said frankly. "If the condition was passed on, it could be similar or potentially more serious. Noonan syndrome includes many different characteristics and disorders and there is no way to know what traits will be passed on and which ones won't. We just don't know enough about it."

"And how soon will you know if I have it?"

"There are certain genetic markers we test for," he said, "and if those are present, then we know with certainty that you have it. But we haven't yet identified all the genetic markers associated with Noonan syndrome, so even if the test is negative, you may still have it."

"So if that happens, how do you diagnose it?"

"We go through all the information you've provided and look at the test results. At that point, it's just a matter of whether or not you have enough traits to make a positive diagnosis. But right now, I'm leaning in that direction."

We shook hands and I left his office in very poor spirits. My mind was all over the place as I continued to think of the day's events and the fact that I might never be able to have healthy children of my own. Then another disturbing thought set in: with this health condition, would I even find a woman to date, marry, and have children with?

As I realized how this diagnosis might impact my quest to find true love, tears welled up in my eyes and lasted my entire drive home.

CHAPTER 3:

FINDING MY RHYTHM

Rhythm is something you either have or don't have, but when you have it, you have it all over.

—Elvis Presley

A week later, I was back in Dr. Ferraro's office.

She looked me in the eye, her features softening with compassion. "I'm afraid the tests we've done so far have not been promising, Rob," she said. "I'm not clearing you for anything until we have more test results."

What did she mean, the tests weren't promising? What was wrong with me? I felt perfectly fine.

Before I had a chance to ask any questions, she looked at her watch. "I'm sorry, we're already running late. You need to get to your cardiac MRI. I'll get the tests scheduled and meet with you next week."

With that, I was on my way to the hospital, where I would be sent through a tube to have my heart photographed.

A beautiful, young radiology technician with shoulder-length blond hair and big blue eyes came to escort me from the hospital waiting room to the room with the MRI machine. I greeted her and made some small talk, but the minute I saw the machine, my mood changed. It looked nothing like the MRI machines I had been through in the past with sports-related injuries. I couldn't believe how enclosed it was.

I was entirely unprepared for the experience. The space inside wasn't any bigger than a hope chest, and I had to be wedged into it.

"Don't worry, Mr. Besecker," the radiology technician said, noticing my apprehension. "It's not as frightening as it looks. When you're inside, it can get pretty loud, so I'm going to give you some headphones to put on. They'll help block the noise and you'll be able to hear my voice, so you won't be alone. I'll be right here, talking you through it."

"How long will I be in there?" I asked her.

"The entire test will take forty-five minutes to an hour," she said, "and you won't be able to move. It's important that you remain perfectly still."

I started to feel frightened just at the thought of being trapped inside that thing. She must have sensed exactly how I felt, because her words flowed in such a soothing tone that with every syllable I began to relax.

"Don't worry," she assured me, "it's perfectly safe. Now, if you start to get nauseous . . ."

As she continued with the details of the procedure and all the possible things that could go wrong—headache, dizziness, chest pain, heart palpitations, you name it, it could happen, all inside that machine—I realized I just wasn't ready for it. There was no way I could let them stick me in that thing.

"I don't think I can do this right now," I said, feeling like such a child.

"Sure you can," she said, putting her hand on my shoulder. "We'll just start slow. How about giving it a try for five minutes? Then I'll pull you out, and when you're ready again, we'll continue. How does that sound?"

She gave me the headphones to put on, and sure enough, there was soothing classical music to fill my head. I was anything but soothed. I was terrified.

I lay down on the table and, before I knew it, I was moving into the machine. I was a fairly muscular and broad-shouldered twenty-eight-year-old man, so it was a tight fit. I felt a lot like I was being squeezed through the barrel of a cannon. My shoulders were squished together, touching the machine on both sides, and there were less than three inches of space between my nose and the enclosure above me.

It was horribly claustrophobic and, despite the headphones, it was loud. Hums, buzzes, and taps competed with the calming sonata coming from the headphones. I felt like I couldn't breathe. I felt like I was being tied up and tortured.

"Let me out!" I said, close to panicking.

Immediately, the table moved and I felt myself returning to the free world.

"I'm sorry, but I can't do this," I said when I was out.

"I understand," the technician said. "How about we try for just two minutes?"

"I guess," I said, "but no more than that. Just let me get myself ready."

We negotiated like that back and forth for some time, and eventually I began to relax. She gave me some water and I took a few sips while silently giving myself a pep talk. *Come on, Rob, don't be a wimp. It's just a test. Nothing bad is going to happen. Just get it done.*

Pretty soon, I'd worked up the energy to try again and I told her I was ready. The table quickly moved back into the long, loud cylinder, and again, after only a minute, I wanted out.

"We're halfway through this image, Rob," she told me in that calming voice that could melt a rock. "Can you just hang on for two more minutes?"

I agreed and lay still. Somehow in the course of those two minutes, I developed the strength to suck it up and deal with it.

"All right, we're pulling you out now," she said.

"You can do another one," I replied, still talking myself into it.

As the test continued, she kept talking to me. "Breathe in, breathe out, hold," she instructed. I hung on to that voice like there was no tomorrow, focusing on every single syllable from the beautiful technician behind the microphone. Her words were a lifeline that calmed me and helped me make it through the next three hours, far longer than I'd ever expected it to take. When it was over, she told me I did a great job, and I felt like a kid looking into the eyes of a hero, proud to have survived a surreal adventure.

I was so relieved to head back to my two-bedroom apartment—which, after being cooped up in that tiny MRI machine, felt like a mansion. But not long after I arrived home, the phone rang. It was Dr. Ferraro.

"We can get you in tomorrow morning for the electrophysiology study," she said.

"Tomorrow morning?"

"Yes, we'd like to get it done right away. Dr. Kluger will do the study. Will you have any family coming with you?"

I was puzzled by her question. "Any family?" I wondered aloud. "Why would I have family coming in? They live in Chicago."

"Well, it's a pretty invasive procedure. You'll need to be sedated, and I'd recommend having family with you."

That's when it finally hit me that I was dealing with something serious. My mind began swirling with a thousand questions. I didn't hear much of anything Dr. Ferraro had to say after that until I heard the word "pacemaker."

"Unless these tests tell us otherwise, I'm afraid we may need to schedule you for a pacemaker or defibrillator by the end of the week."

Then she rattled off a bunch of possible complications, but I didn't hear any of them. I couldn't think—my mind had gone numb. Everything was coming at me so fast, I couldn't process it all. I needed more time, but from the way she was talking, it didn't seem I had any choice. She was bound and determined to find out what was wrong with my heart.

After Dr. Ferraro finished explaining everything, I immediately called Chris.

"Hey, sis," I said, "do you know what an electrophysiology study is?"

"Holy shit!" she said. "It's a test where they check out the electrical activity and conduction pathways of your heart. Why, do they want you to have one of those?"

"Yes, they're making me take a whole slew of tests. All I want is to be cleared to get off the beta blockers so I can join the service, but now they're saying something about the possibility of a pacemaker or defibrillator."

"A pacemaker or defibrillator? My god, this is serious. When do they want you to do it?"

"Maybe by the end of the week, but they want the electrophysiology study done first thing tomorrow morning," I told her.

"Do you want me to come?" she asked.

I knew if Chris was willing to leave Chicago that night and join me at the hospital, things must be bad.

Before I could answer, she asked another question: "Have they told you anything about the study?"

"They haven't said much; are you familiar with it?"

"They insert catheters in your groin to measure your heart's electrical pathways," she explained. "It's invasive, and they'll puncture your skin with a needle to insert the catheters through your groin. It's really uncomfortable."

My mind was spinning with so many fears that I could barely hear what Chris was saying, but the procedure was sounding more and more frightening the more she described it.

"Then, they'll press a couple of electromagnets against you," she continued. "They're pretty big, but you'll be unconscious so you won't feel them. The doctor will stimulate different regions of your heart to try to replicate the arrhythmias you've been having. That gives them a better idea of what's going on with your heart."

"You mean they're going to stop my heart on purpose?"

Chris laughed, though we both knew it was no joking matter. "Well, yeah, sort of. But only for a second, just to see what's going on."

"How are they going to do that?"

"With electrical current, usually. If that doesn't work, then they'll use drugs or an ablation."

I was speechless, paralyzed with thought.

"Look," Chris continued, "let me call work and tell them I can't come in tomorrow, book a flight, and pack. We'll talk later."

It has always been difficult for me to admit to being vulnerable, but I was really scared and needed support now more than ever. Once we hung up, I wrote a mass email to my friends and family, updating them on what was happening and asking for their thoughts and prayers.

I pushed the "send" button and just stared at the walls.

This shit was getting real.

I picked up Chris at the airport later that night. The next morning, we drove to the hospital, doing our best to chat like any brother and sister heading off on a family errand: "How've you been?" "Dating anybody?" "Hear from Mom and Dad lately?"

Though I continued to act like I had everything under control, I had no idea what was coming. My goal of joining the military seemed like a distant memory, and I was reminded of having to give up my dream of playing college football because of my damaged body. How much more devastation could my body withstand?

After I got checked in at the hospital, Chris stayed with me as long as she could. Eventually, I was ushered into the prep room and had to say good-bye. She assured me she'd be nearby and would be checking on my progress.

I spent the entire day suffering through the electrophysiology study performed by Dr. Kluger, an electrophysiologist Dr. Ferraro had studied under at Hartford Hospital.

The only thing worse than the procedure itself was when it was over.

Once the catheters were removed from my femoral artery and the anesthetic had worn off, I had to lie perfectly immobile, not even lifting my head, for six hours. That was hell. I lay on that bed wanting to turn over, to stretch, to scratch and itch, but I couldn't. All I could do was lie there.

"I'd like to keep you here for the next few days, Rob," Dr. Kluger said. "Tomorrow, we'll do some more MRI testing, a tilt test, and a stress test."

I nodded, wishing I could just go home. Instead, I would spend the next three nights being woken up every other hour to have my blood pressure taken and my heart checked. I felt healthy and strong, but clearly a good night's sleep was not in the picture.

Chris hung out with me at the hospital and kept me calm while I asked her a million questions. The better I understood what was going on with my heart and what my options were, the more prepared I'd be to make the right choices about my care.

▲▲ ▲▲ ▲▲

The next morning, I was back in the cardiac MRI tube—which, after the electrophysiology study, wasn't nearly as bad as it had been the first time around. I was also relaxed about the upcoming tilt test, which sounded about as stressful as watching TV: they'd put me on a slightly tilted table and have me stand in place. That, at least, was something I could handle.

Dr. Kluger, a nice guy, administered the tilt test; this time he was accompanied by an equally friendly advanced nurse practitioner named Danette.

"All right, Rob," Danette instructed me. "Go ahead and lie down on this table and relax."

She gestured to what looked like an examination table, except that it had big black straps dangling from the sides and a footboard.

I hoisted myself onto it and lay down as four or five other people— Dr. Kluger, another doctor, a couple of nurses, and Danette—all watched.

"Okay," I said once I was lying down and another series of electrodes had been stuck all over my chest. "Now what?"

The table slowly swiveled until I was nearly upright but tilted back ever so slightly.

"Now stay calm," Dr. Kluger said.

All I could think was, *Is he nuts? This is nothing.* My feet were resting on the footboard. I was exerting no energy.

"Stay calm, Rob; stay calm."

"I don't get it," I said. "What's the purpose of this?"

"We just want to see how your heart responds," he explained.

"When was the last time you had a blackout?" Danette asked, taking notes and checking on the monitors as she talked.

"When you called me in from the waiting room," I said, "but it was just for a second."

Dr. Kluger nodded and kept taking notes while watching the monitors.

So I just stood there, strapped down and relaxed, having a nice conversation with the medical team, all the while thinking, *Why am I strapped to this thing? This is ridiculous.*

Five minutes passed this way. And then, all of a sudden, I felt strange.

"I'm starting to feel a little awkward," I said.

"What do you mean by awkward?" Dr. Kluger asked.

"I don't know, just funny—"

A dizzy spell came over me, cutting short my explanation. This one was worse than the others because I couldn't sit, I couldn't grab hold of anything. I was just strapped in, unable to move, while they stood around me and watched. What had been perfectly relaxing a moment before suddenly felt like torture.

"This is it," I said as everything grew dark around the edges and I felt myself blacking out. "It's happening; it's worse than before!"

The next thing I knew, I was lying horizontally.

"What happened?" I asked.

"You passed out," Danette said. "We knew it was going to happen pretty quickly after you mentioned feeling lightheaded earlier."

"You did that to me on purpose?" I asked, stunned.

"Yes. We needed to see how your heart would respond to a change in blood pressure," she explained. "It helps us to determine the cause of the blackouts you've been having." She glanced at her notes. "Your heart didn't perform well on any of the tests. It just isn't beating properly. Sometimes it races uncontrollably, and other times it doesn't beat fast enough. We're going to have to install a pacemaker to keep your heart beating at a proper rhythm. I'd also recommend a defibrillator, which can send an electrical shock to the heart and prevent sudden cardiac death. We can insert a dual-function device, one that will be both a pacemaker and a defibrillator."

"I strongly advise the ICD as a precautionary measure," Dr. Kluger interjected.

I looked at him. "An ICD?" "The defibrillator. Having the dual function is the safest option."

"You mean I'll have to have heart surgery?"

"Yes," Dr. Kluger said. "I'll make a small incision in your chest and surround the device with tissue under your skin to hold it in place. Then we'll thread the wires through a vein to your heart. You'll be sedated; you won't feel a thing."

"I don't understand," I said, shaking my head. "What exactly is a defibrillator? How is that different from a pacemaker?"

"Essentially, a pacemaker provides electrical impulses to the heart to keep it beating and regulate the rhythm. A defibrillator is more of an emergency backup in case the heart goes into a ventricular tachycardia or ventricular fibrillation. You know those big electrical paddles that they use to get a heart beating again when someone's heart stops?"

I nodded.

"Well, the defibrillator is like that, but it's very small and installed inside your body. If your heart goes into a life-threatening rhythm, the defibrillator will give your heart an electrical jolt to get it beating again."

"And that's what you think I need?"

"Yes. You need a pacemaker. We are recommending the defibrillator as an extra precaution. It's a relatively simple surgery."

It didn't sound simple at all, but it was looking as if I had no choice.

"I don't understand." I frowned. "Why do I need both? Is that common? My mom and uncle both have pacemakers, but they don't have defibrillators."

"None of this is common for someone your age. Rarely do we see anyone in your shape who needs one, but after reviewing the tests, we all agree that the only way to be safe is to implant a defibrillator."

I nodded. I had the body of a young athlete but the heart of an old man. Why? What had I done wrong? I was speechless; all I wanted to do was go back to my room in the hospital and think.

▲▲ ▲▲ ▲▲

My sister was with me when Dr. Ferraro came in a short while later.

"Let's get you scheduled for surgery right away," she said.

"What do you mean by right away?" I asked, wanting nothing more than to go home and sleep in my own bed.

"Hopefully we can get you in first thing in the morning," she said.

The doctors wanted me to make a decision about my body and health with no real time to think about it. I wasn't ready.

"How long have I had this problem?" I asked.

"Probably all your life," Dr. Ferraro said.

"Then the chances of something happening and me dying are not any greater now than they were two weeks ago, before we knew any of this, right?"

"Yes, that's right."

"Robby," Chris said, laying a hand on my shoulder, "you should just go ahead and have it done now. You're already here, it's clear you need the device, and I have to get back home to my kids."

"No," I said. "I can't make this decision right now. I need more time."

My body was about to be changed forever and I needed more information before deciding which device—just a pacemaker or a combination defibrillator-pacemaker—I should let the doctor implant in me.

After lengthy discussions with my doctors, I felt better informed. With a pacemaker, they told me, the scar would be smaller and the device hardly noticeable. With the defibrillator-pacemaker ICD combo, I'd have a bigger scar and the device would protrude from my chest like a pack of cigarettes, but it also could be a bigger lifesaver. At the end of our conversation, I assured them that I'd do some research and make a decision as soon as possible. Then I checked out of the hospital. Since I wasn't allowed to drive, one of my friends picked me up, and we took Chris to the airport in an awkward silence.

▲▲ ▲▲ ▲▲

I have always tried to look at the positive over the negative, the opportunities that come when things don't go as planned, the door that opens when another one closes. However, after being told just a few weeks shy of my twenty-ninth birthday that I would need a miniature set of jumper cables planted in my chest, it was hard to find any silver lining.

At least I was in control, somewhat. I'd made the decision to take an active role in my treatment and not just accept what I was told without more information. I went online and began to research everything I could about living with a defibrillator and pacemaker.

▲▲ ▲▲ ▲▲

Danette called me the next day. She was aware of my concerns and was offering me the opportunity to speak to someone who might be able to help with my decision. That weekend, I met Glen, an avid hockey player who was six years older than me. Although his heart conditions were far different from mine, he had a defibrillator in his chest and seemed to understand my struggles. Talking with Glen and his wife helped me a great deal in making my final decision. Glen even let me see and touch the device to help me feel more comfortable with what it was like.

After that weekend, I called Drs. Kluger and Ferraro to let them know that I would move forward with the ICD surgery.

My dad and Chris flew in from Chicago for the surgery, so I had family by my side—not to mention tons of comments, cards, and thoughtful prayers from the many loved ones from all over the country and world I'd reached out to when I sent that mass email.

Some friends and coworkers had arranged to assist with my driving, shopping, and cooking needs while I recovered so I wouldn't have to worry about any of my day-to-day responsibilities. I had a recovery team in place. I was blessed.

I also felt confident that I was in good hands with my doctors. Dr. Ferraro had studied under Dr. Kluger and they had a great relationship. I knew they would make an excellent team and I trusted their abilities.

▲▲ ▲▲ ▲▲

I woke up from surgery feeling like a rabid pit bull had taken a bite out of my chest and a bulldozer had come along and parked on top of it. I also woke up thanking God for more blessings than I could count.

Still, I knew I wasn't cured. Dr. Kluger had taken four tissue samples from my heart during the surgery and gotten a biopsy done on them, and all four had tested as scar tissue, as if I had suffered a heart attack at some point. My heart was damaged, defective. Just how long it would keep beating was anybody's guess, and knowing that I could get jolted with an electrical shock at any moment wasn't exactly comforting.

I was hurting and, for the first time in my life, I was face to face with my own mortality.

I might never make it to thirty. I might never find true love and get married. I might never be able to play sports again.

My mind swirled with the worst possible thoughts and fears as I kept touching my chest, feeling the newly implanted defibrillator.

What is my life going to be like? What's my life expectancy? When will the surgical wound heal and the pain stop throbbing?

When I was released from the hospital the next day, I received some answers.

"No driving for two weeks. And don't shower or bathe for another four days," the nurse told me. "And no lifting with your left arm. Here, wear this," she said, handing me a sling. "This will keep you from moving it. Don't lift your arm above your head for one month—otherwise you might displace one of the wires placed in your heart."

"Can I at least carry my football home?" I asked, hoisting up the new football some friends had gotten signed by Chicago Bears legend Dick Butkus, arguably the greatest linebacker there ever was—whom my dad also happened to play against in high school.

She smiled. "Sure, just don't go playing any games with it. Here, you need to carry this defibrillator identification card in your wallet. That way, if there's any problem, the EMTs will know you have one. And when you fly, be sure to tell the airline personnel that you have a defibrillator and pacemaker."

"Okay. Anything else? Can I be near microwave ovens? Use a cell phone?"

"You can microwave all you want. You can use your cell phone, just don't place it directly on your chest where the device is. You shouldn't go through the metal detector at airport screenings. Have the agents do a pat-down, and if they use a wand, ask them not to put it directly over the device. Oh, and there's one more thing you can't do."

"What's that?" I asked, tensing, expecting her to say, "No more sex."

"No more MRIs."

I almost laughed. It was the last thing I expected her to say.

"That's it? Just no more MRIs?" No more squeezing into a claustrophobia-inducing machine and listening to another chorus of Pachelbel?

I smiled. There was a silver lining after all.

CHAPTER 4:

GOING THROUGH CHANGE

It is not the strongest of the species that survives, nor the most intelligent. It is the one that is most adaptable to change.

—Charles Darwin

Though every cloud has a silver lining, it was hard to see the positive side of the tragedy that upended my world the following year—especially after I had worked so hard to pull myself out of the funk I fell into following my ICD implant surgery.

After I was released from the hospital in May 2003, I felt like I was on house arrest. I wasn't able to drive or exercise, I had to avoid sunlight and water, and sometimes it felt like the only time I ever got out was for another doctor's visit or follow-up testing at the hospital. I was in pain, lonely, and depressed. What ultimately helped me get through this turbulent time was by connecting with other ICD recipients and participating in a cardiac support group at the hospital. They helped me to see that I was not alone in my struggles.

As the summer progressed and my restrictions were lifted, I realized that my fear that life was going to slow to a crawl had proven groundless. I began to exercise and enjoy the summer weather as soon as I could, and as I did I discovered that my heart was no longer limiting my progress. If anything, I was stronger and happier than I'd been in a long time.

▲▲ ▲▲ ▲▲

In September, I was transferred from Connecticut to Indianapolis with a consumer and non-aerospace-and-defense-related division of the company. I was now only a three-hour drive from my family and friends in Chicago, and yet I hardly saw them—I was too consumed with work.

The professional development and regular business travel my new job required was fun, but the sixty-hour workweeks were daunting. In my quest for balance, I took some much-needed vacation time in March and traveled to Las Vegas.

The minute my plane landed at McCarran International Airport, I turned on my phone to check my voice messages. There was only one, from my mom, sharing news that would alter our family forever.

"Robby," she said in a serious tone, "you need to come home right away."

I froze. In that sliver of a second, my mind raced straight to the most horrible possibilities.

Then she said matter-of-factly, "Rusty died."

My stomach sank to my feet. I got off the plane, numb with shock. My thirty-eight-year-old brother was dead. *How can this be?*

I immediately arranged to turn right around and get on the next flight to Chicago, a red-eye. I arrived home exhausted and still in shock, even though I guess you could say Rusty's death wasn't entirely unexpected.

Rusty was always a hellion. As a child he was labeled as "hyperactive," but by the time he reached high school he had been officially diagnosed as a paranoid schizophrenic. As he got older, the schizophrenia got even more severe. Rusty was in and out of jails and institutions, became addicted to drugs and alcohol, and was so mentally ill that he was incoherent at times—but all of us in the family still loved him.

Every time I went back home, the first thing I did was call Rusty and take him out to lunch. He'd be dressed in multiple layers of clothing, a knit cap pulled over his ears even in the blazing hot summer, and just the look of him, so large and confused and overly dressed, would cause people to stare. But I didn't care what other people thought. He was still my big brother.

"So, Rusty, did you catch the game last week?" I'd ask him over lunch.

Rusty was a passionate sports fan and we debated a lot about our favorite teams, the Bears and the Cubs. We'd also chat about the family, the weather, how he was doing, and how I was doing, and then I'd pay the bill and we'd go.

However limited our visits were, they drew us closer, and we had a loving bond. He knew he was safe with me, and I knew I was safe with him.

Sadly, though, he wasn't safe with himself. He had been struggling with drugs and alcohol for years, and as his addictions and delusions increased, there wasn't much my parents could do to help him. Addiction is a bad enough disease; combined with paranoid schizophrenia, it's even worse.

When Rusty began losing control, my dad got into the habit of checking on him daily. Then one day, he couldn't reach him. He went to Rusty's apartment and rang the bell but there was no answer, and my dad had a feeling something was terribly wrong. He found the building manager and got him to open up the door to the apartment. That's where he found Rusty, dead on the floor after suffering a heart attack from a drug overdose. Rusty had been using cocaine and drinking quite heavily, and apparently he had consumed a great deal right before he died.

My dad was devastated. He always had been a stoic man, and the only emotion he usually allowed himself to express was his anger. However, with the death of my brother, I saw for the first time how deeply he loved his children. He could hardly make any decisions about Rusty's wake and funeral, and my mom was inconsolable. So Chris, Cindy, and I stepped in and made all the arrangements.

Through it all, I was utterly stunned. Up to that point, all my concern had been focused on the possibility that I would have an early death, yet it was my brother we were burying. The stone-cold reality of death slapped me hard. Over the course of my life I had been through the deaths of an uncle who died of an epileptic seizure, my beloved grandfather, and my grandmothers, both of whom died in 1997. But this death was different. This was my brother. Even more so than when I'd had my defibrillator installed, I came face to face with how suddenly and swiftly death can strike us down.

I gave the eulogy at Rusty's funeral, which helped me to feel a sense of closure about his life, albeit a painful one.

Rusty's life had been tragic, but that didn't make his death any less tragic. I watched from afar as my parents settled into their grief in their own private ways—my father by withdrawing, my mother by falling apart—and, just as I had with my heart, I felt powerless to do anything.

▲▲ ▲▲ ▲▲

Although it was hard to find any silver lining in my brother's death, tragedy can bring people together. After Rusty's death, both my parents were up for doing something with the rest of us as a family. Though my dad was deathly afraid of flying and rarely traveled, he decided he would do so this time so we all could take a family vacation: a cruise to Alaska.

It became clear on the trip that grief was not my father's only struggle. For years he had battled leg and back pain and had difficulty walking short distances, something we had always attributed to a flesh-eating disease that had nearly cost him his life.

It revealed itself when I was sixteen years old, just after he'd come home from a fishing trip. My dad was in his room sitting in a chair with his leg propped up on a pillow, and I noticed that it was red and swollen.

"What's wrong with your leg, Dad?" I asked.

"Oh, it's nothing," he said. "I probably just got some damn bug bite. It's sore as hell, though."

"You should get that checked out," I said, concerned. My father never complained of pain, so I knew he was hurting. "Want me to take you to the hospital?"

"Nah," he grumbled, "I don't need to go to any damn hospital. I'll be fine."

The following morning, I saw that his leg had swollen up even worse. It was dark red and purple, and he was grimacing in pain with every movement.

"Enough is enough," I told him. "I'm taking you to the hospital."

As he protested, I sat down on the edge of the bed, pulled his arm around my shoulder, and hoisted him up. Then I practically carried him down the stairs and left him leaning against the wall by the door as I got the car. By the time I got back to the house, he'd maneuvered his way to the front porch and fallen. I picked him back up and literally carried him to the car and rushed him to the hospital.

"Your father has a bacterial disease called necrotizing fasciitis," the doctor explained. "It's a rare but serious disease that destroys the skin and underlying tissues. We can remove the dead tissue and contaminated substances from the wound and treat him with antibiotics and other drugs, but there's no guarantee he won't lose his leg. You did the right thing bringing him in when you did; if he had waited another hour, he would have died."

They immediately took my dad to surgery, after which he was admitted into intensive care with septic shock from the infection that had spread through his whole body. When I saw him in the ICU he didn't say much, but I knew he was grateful I'd brought him in and saved his life.

My father recovered after multiple surgeries and skin grafts, but his leg continued to be weak, and the effects of the disease seemed unrelenting, even after all these years. He was often in pain. And as he tried moving around during that family trip to Alaska, it became clear just how weak he really was. He spent most of his time on the ship, and when he did venture onto land, he was slow and unsteady.

One day we went on a fishing excursion to catch some salmon, and though my dad loved fishing and we had a great time, for me the day was somewhat tainted. It was devastating to see how much my once-athletic father, a former football star who received a full sports scholarship to Purdue University, was struggling as he walked to and from the dock.

Watching him limp along, I was reminded of the second time I had saved my father's life.

I was seventeen years old and he had asked me to help him push his old, beat-up, two-door Buick to a gas station about 200 yards from our house because the transmission was out. I was doing the heavy pushing of the car from behind while my dad was pushing near the driver's door and steering.

We were going up a bit of a hill, and at one point, the car began to roll backward. I warned my dad to get in the car, but he was too weak to lift his legs in and fell as he tried to do so. Seeing that the car was going to roll back over him, I abandoned my post, ran to his side, and—just as he closed his eyes and prepared for the worst—grabbed him under the armpits and yanked him out of harm's way.

In that moment, I had earned my father's pride and respect.

I wished I could have been there for Rusty the way I'd been there for my dad in the past. After my dad found him and went home to tell my mom, my parents and both sisters had gone to see his body before the coroners picked it up and carried out of his apartment. As morbid as it may sound, it hurt that I hadn't been there with my family for that moment of grieving together.

Rusty's death, overall, was hard for me to accept and had me questioning where I was going in my own life. Ever since reading *Romeo and Juliet* in high school, I had been in love with the concept of love, and I had been seeking true love my entire adult life. Yet here I was, thirty years old, and what did I have to show for it? I had no family of my own, no wife and no children.

I was involved in a long-distance relationship with a woman named Vivian at the time. She lived in Orlando; we worked for the same company and had met at a business meeting in Indianapolis. Vivian was successful and fun. We squabbled a bit, but with Rusty's death, I decided it was time to put a real effort into the relationship. When I was offered a new job in Orlando, Vivian asked me to come live with her, and I accepted.

▲▲ ▲▲ ▲▲

Initially, the move to Orlando was exciting—living in a nice home, having a new job, and enjoying the great weather. However, my relationship with Vivian had been rocky from the very beginning. With all that added closeness and all that lost solitude, it wasn't long before we were arguing daily. As much as I wanted the relationship to work, I had serious doubts about our future together.

I had to put those doubts aside, though, when I was forced to focus on my health once again. It had been one year since I'd had the pacemaker and defibrillator implanted, and—almost to the day of that anniversary, as if the damn things were programmed to expire once the warranty was up—I began to have a series of alarming incidents.

The real problems began when I had to fly back up to Hartford to see Dr. Kluger for a checkup on my ICD. Despite many battles with insurance, I wanted to continue seeing my team of physicians in Connecticut, who provided excellent care and were familiar with my medical conditions.

"Hmm . . ." Dr. Kluger said, reviewing the results from my ICD check. "Looks like you've had a couple of incidents in the last two months. Do you remember them?"

"Really?" I was surprised. "When were they?"

"You had one on June 3rd that lasted twenty-four minutes, and another on July 17th that lasted nineteen hours."

"Really?" I couldn't believe it. Maybe he meant nineteen minutes? If my heart had been having problems for nineteen hours, wouldn't I have known it?

"Yes, Rob. Your heart was in stress for nineteen hours that day. That was last weekend. Do you remember what you were doing?"

"I was having a garage sale," I told him. "I was just sitting in a lawn chair, selling old VHS tapes. I know I felt horrible all day long, but I didn't think it was cardiac-related."

"Have you been taking your medication?" Dr. Kluger asked.

"Yes, I always take my medication," I said, beginning to worry. If I didn't even know when my heart was in distress, how could I possibly control it?

Other than changing my medication, there wasn't much else Dr. Kluger could do at that point. Through remote monitoring of my device, I could send readings of my heart to him and Dr. Ferraro whenever I felt uncomfortable, and I assured him I would do so.

I returned to Florida feeling depressed and discouraged. My heart was out of control.

Then, a couple weeks later, I received a distressing call from Dr. Ferraro.

"Rob, I want you to get back up here right away," she said.

"Why? What's wrong?" I asked her. "I feel fine."

"You're not fine. You've been in AFib five days in a row."

I knew that five days in AFib wasn't good. The longer your heart stays in atrial fibrillation or any other abnormal rhythm, the harder it is to correct it. It was not something I could ignore.

"I want to get you scheduled for a cardioversion right away," she said, referring to the controlled procedure where an electronic shock is sent to your heart, either through your ICD or an external device, to bring your heart back to a normal rhythm.

I hung up the phone, stunned and silent.

The day I was supposed to fly back to Connecticut, Hurricane Charley struck. I had never been through a natural disaster like that before. The interesting thing is that, as Vivian and I spent the entire night huddled in the hallway next to the bathroom, the only spot clear of any windows that could break, wearing my raincoat and shoes and clutching a radio by my side, I wasn't thinking about dying or even about missing my appointment in Connecticut—I was thinking about my buddy Anton, who had been my roommate and closest friend in Connecticut after we attended Purdue together for our MBA. He was getting married, and I was going to miss his wedding. And it wasn't the first time that had happened: the year before, I'd missed my fraternity brother Rob's wedding because it was the weekend after I had my device installed.

The entire experience gave me the feeling that I was being excluded from the most precious experiences and rituals of life. Whether it was my damaged body or a hurricane, it seemed the universe didn't want me to share in the joy of those who meant the most to me. I just wanted to be like everyone else, but fate didn't seem to be allowing that to happen.

▲▲ ▲▲ ▲▲

When the hurricane finally lifted, I caught the first flight to Connecticut—where, coincidentally, I ran into Anton's family at the airport. They were returning to Georgia after the wedding. It was a bittersweet moment: I was delighted to see them, but it served as another reminder that I'd missed out on the festivities.

Later that evening, Chris and Cindy flew to Hartford to be with me for the procedure. It was scheduled for the next day, and I was too nervous to go to sleep that night, so we spent the evening at the casino, trying to block out reality. The next morning, though, was when the real gamble began.

Before going in for the cardioversion, it was necessary to monitor my heart with a TEE, a transesophageal echocardiogram. The last thing I remember before the anesthesia kicked in was the nasty, cement-tasting stuff they sprayed in my throat to numb it, then a tube being worked down my throat as if to gag me.

When I woke up after the cardioversion procedure was complete, I was in a hospital room and already feeling much better now that my heart was in normal sinus rhythm—though I sure was sore. I tossed and turned in the hospital bed, wanting to leave but knowing I couldn't.

That night, as the buzzes and beeps of the health-monitoring equipment in the hospital began to quiet and the lights in my room were turned off, I tried to sleep. It didn't come easily, even though I was so groggy from the medications and lingering anesthesia. After lying on my right side for a while thinking about everything that was happening, I tried turning to my left and got a sharp pain in my chest. The pain wasn't constant, but it kept coming back whenever I moved or took a deep breath. So I lay flat on my back and worried, thinking about what I would do if my device went off. I also started to tear up, fearful of what could be happening to me. For the first time, I wondered if I might be dying.

It was time to reevaluate my life and make some changes; otherwise, I could die just like Rusty did, suddenly and all alone.

CHAPTER 5:

HEROES AND DETOURS

I think a hero is an ordinary individual who finds the strength to persevere and endure in spite of overwhelming obstacles.

—Christopher Reeve

ll too often, turbulent times lead people to defensiveness and the criticism of others, but I wanted more introspection. *What can I do differently?* I began to reflect on my past, specifically when I was in high school, before the physical limitations of my body took me off course. My mind wandered to a time when a couple students from a nearby community college came to interview several people from my high school for a documentary they were putting together for a class project. As a popular student athlete, I was one of eight students asked to participate in the video and answer a question on who was my hero and why.

Throughout the day, I gave the question some serious thought. Given my passion for sports, I considered options like my favorite linebacker,

Dick Butkus, for his grit and ability to play through pain, and Walter Payton, who played thirteen seasons through injury while only missing one game his rookie season. I also considered presidents like George Washington and Abraham Lincoln, military leaders like George Patton and Douglas MacArthur, and even my dad, for good measure.

It was nearly the end of the day when I was called into an office for the interview. As I arrived, one of the college students greeted me.

"Hi Rob!" he began. "Thank you for agreeing to participate in the documentary we are creating. Do you have any questions?"

"No thanks, it seems pretty straightforward," I answered.

"We're just going to ask you one question and video your response. The others have all finished, and they will be in the room along with my partner for your interview."

"Sounds good," I said.

He opened the door and we walked into the room.

As the camera light came on with all the others watching, the interviewer asked, "Rob, what is your definition of a hero?"

"Someone who has overcome great barriers and continues to help others," I began. "Someone who puts the greater good before individual achievement, and follows a moral path despite obstacles along the way."

I continued for a moment, confident in my words, which seemed to flow with ease.

As I concluded, the guy behind the camera nodded his head with approval and, in a matter-of-fact tone, asked, "So, who is your hero?"

Suddenly, none of the names I had considered throughout the day seemed to fit the definition I had given—but another name occurred to me that did. Without hesitation, I said, "Jesus Christ."

Everyone in the room—including me—was shocked by my answer. Though I had never been a particularly religious person prior to that moment, the experience has permanently stuck with me, and it was the starting point of my spiritual journey.

▲▲ ▲▲ ▲▲

Following the cardioversion, I did everything I could to have a healthier heart. I ran and worked out even more, stopped drinking all alcoholic and caffeinated beverages, and modified my diet. I also prayed. With my health concerns and the emotional turmoil I was facing, I wanted to feel spiritually connected now more than ever. I was looking for the kind of connection that not even my doctors, friends, or family could provide, something to help me deal with the chaos in my life.

All I could think about was how my whole life had been derailed. It felt as if one minute I was perfectly healthy and watching TV with my family, and the next minute my heart was galloping straight out of my chest and my whole future was being called into question. I'd been told my heart could stop at any moment. I'd been told I had a rare congenital disorder that could be passed on to my children. I'd moved to Florida for what had soon been revealed to be a deteriorating and unhealthy relationship. My brother had died, and I'd had two mind-altering cardiac procedures. In less than two years, I'd experienced enough stressors to last a lifetime. How many more were in my future? Did I even *have* a future? At any second I could just be gone—and the world would go on without me.

I set out to find a purpose, *my* purpose. My first move was to check out a church my friends from the softball league I'd joined in Orlando had told me about.

As I looked around at the congregation, I saw so many faces glowing. Children fidgeted in their seats, bored out of their minds; men snuck glances at their Blackberries; and women scolded them both, gesturing to pay attention.

Do they realize how quickly life can change? I wondered. *Do they know that at any moment their own lives could change, just like mine?*

I wanted to reach my full potential in life. I thought I had done the right things—I ate healthy, worked out, and avoided alcohol, cigarettes, and drugs—yet it seemed that no matter how hard I tried, that wasn't going to happen.

I'm kind and caring and nice to people, aren't I? So why can't I have a long life like everyone else? For that matter, why did Rusty have to die? Sure, he was flawed, but he was loved. Did he really have to die in an instant, all alone? Will that happen to me?

As those thoughts whirled around in my head, the sermon slowly began to reach me. The pastor was talking about detours.

"Have you ever been traveling on the highway and seen a sign that says, 'Detour'?" he asked. "We've all seen those signs. And when we do, we think, *Well that's just great. That's the last thing I need. Now I'm going to be late. I might get lost. I might never reach my destination. I hadn't planned on a detour.*" He chuckled. "None of us plan on detours, and none of us are happy when we see them. However, sometimes when we take a detour, we are pleasantly surprised. We might find ourselves discovering a new and more scenic route. We might stop at a restaurant we'd otherwise have missed and have a wonderful meal or meet someone new. Furthermore, we might never know what tragedy we missed by taking a detour. Had there been no detour and we'd continued on the road we were traveling, we may have found ourselves stuck in traffic, run out of gas, been in a serious car accident, or even worse. Those are misfortunes we were spared but never knew were up ahead—because we took a detour."

I was riveted by the sermon. His words spoke directly to my heart. It was as if that message had been created just for me. I was no longer staring at the congregation; I was listening intently to the meaning of the message being delivered.

"And just as traveling on the highway forces us to take detours when we least expect it, traveling on the roads of life will inevitably bring us detours," he continued. "We get divorced, lose our job, our home is foreclosed, a family member dies. We had never prepared for these events, but here they are."

We break our backs, our hearts may not work properly, I thought as he spoke. *We discover we could die at any moment.* Yes, life had handed me its share of lemons. What did it mean? What was I supposed to learn from it all? I leaned in, as if moving a few inches closer might help me obtain the answers more quickly. My heart, I realized, had become my own personal detour—the life detour I was being forced to take, whether I wanted to or not.

"When the Apostle Paul suffered the pain of a thorn in his flesh, he was angry. He had no time for suffering; he had work to carry out. He called on the Lord to remove the thorn, and the Lord replied, 'My grace is sufficient.' Paul was at first incredulous—how could the Lord ignore his pleas? His goals were glorious, his heart magnanimous. He was serving the Lord, yet the Lord did nothing to ease his pain and suffering." The pastor's voice carried, loud and clear, through the church. "In time, Paul came to see that only through his suffering could he be humbled enough to carry out his work. He had been so filled with pride for his good work that he was blinded to the path he was on. The thorn in his flesh was a reminder that he, too, was human, and that just as all humans endure suffering at some time in their lives, so must he."

Those words struck a chord with me. All this time, I'd been asking, *Why is this happening?* Now, however, I realized that we all have our individual struggles to move through. This was my burden to tackle with grace.

"And once Paul was humbled by this truth, he realized that a pure life does not mean that it will be free of suffering. To live a pure life, one must recognize suffering will come in many ways. But what one *makes* of that suffering will truly test our grace with God."

These words buried themselves in my soul, igniting a thousand fires of clarity within me. Like Paul's thorn, my damaged heart could strengthen me. It could be an opportunity. I still had no idea how or in what way, but I knew the pastor's message was exactly what I needed to hear. As he brought the sermon to a close, I came to see that, like everyone, I had a destiny to fulfill. It wasn't necessarily the fate I had planned for, but it was mine to discover.

"Let us then remember that when life presents us with a detour, our place is not to curse God or our families or our friends or our bosses or our fate for having forced us from the road we were traveling and placing us on another road we hadn't planned to travel. It is up to us how we travel down that new and unexpected road. We can travel our new route, cursing and wailing and checking our watches, checking to see how much time we are losing, complaining about what sites we are missing for having been forced off one road and onto another." The pastor's voice softened, his fiery tone growing quiet. "Or we can open our eyes to the new sites, the new people, the new discoveries that are now before us. These are the humbling and exciting gifts that we never would have received had we not taken a detour. And these gifts are for us to receive with grace and wisdom, not rage and ignorance. The detour may not be our choice, but how we travel that detour is entirely up to each of us.

For all of us will face detours in our lives, just as Paul came to realize that not even he, an apostle, would be spared. God will not spare you either, so be humbled by the detours up ahead, and He will make sure that you will reach your destiny. It may not be the destiny you'd planned for yourself. But it will be the destiny God has planned for you. Amen."

I left the church a new man. I had entered as an angry, confused soul, cursing my broken back and weak heart, which I believed were preventing me from pursuing my dreams. I walked out with the realization that how I responded to the circumstances before me was completely within my control. I was in charge of how I moved forward, and I was ready to take on the world.

All my life I'd set goals for myself, and for the most part I'd achieved them. Being goal-oriented gave me purpose—yet some of those goals were slipping past me. I'd made it a goal to get a scholarship for college, and I'd achieved that. I'd made it a goal to get an MBA from a top-ranked school, and I'd achieved that as well. I'd also made it a goal to get married by the time I was twenty-five, and have kids before I was thirty. Those two goals had eluded me.

I'd seen all the missed goals as failures, beating myself up for a history of failed relationships, for breaking my back and not playing college football, for having a damaged heart and not joining the service—as if those things were my fault and within my control.

Now I realized they weren't failures at all—they were detours and opportunities. As long as I lived in the past and viewed them as failures, I would be stuck and unable to move forward. But in identifying them as detours, I could restore purpose to my life. I still had the ability to do something special; I was just taking an unexpected journey to get there.

As for my damaged body? Well, despite all its flaws, I realized it was an amazing creation, and within it lay a valuable message unto itself. Just consider the body parts that aid with the five senses: First, there are the eyes, located at the top of the face and directed forward so we can see what's in front of us. Next are the ears, cupped forward, offering the ability to hear noise directed at us. Taste comes from our mouth and tongue, also facing ahead. Our sense of smell comes from our nose, which again is pointed forward. Finally, our fifth sense is touch, and even our fingers are generally directed forward, reaching for what's in front of us. Even the shoulders, chest, reproductive organs, and feet, all face forward. There is only one part of the human anatomy that is pointed backward, and it is responsible for the removal of unnecessary entities that should be left behind.

The message of the human body clearly translates to letting go of the past, focusing on the present, and surveying the future. After hearing the pastor's powerful message, I realized that's what I needed to do myself.

My new outlook on living turned my life around, and it was clear my relationship with Vivian did not fit on the road ahead. Detours were one thing; knowingly traveling in the wrong direction was another. As soon as I realized this, I ended things with her.

▲▲ ▲▲ ▲▲

After only a year and a half in Florida, my detours took me to a job selling cholesterol-lowering medications for a pharmaceutical company back in Connecticut. Given my own health problems, which included issues with high cholesterol, and given my family's medical history, I felt working in healthcare was a calling.

I wasn't the only one heading on an unexpected detour.

Not long after our Alaskan cruise, my mother called with devastating news: my father had been diagnosed with an adult-onset form of muscular dystrophy that was causing his muscles to slowly waste away. All those problems he'd been having with his legs now began to make perfect sense.

It turned out my dad had myotonic dystrophy type 2 (DM2), a form of muscular dystrophy that was multisystemic and could affect everything, including his muscles, eyes, pancreas, heart, and other organs. Adult-onset DM2 is considered a rare form of MD; fortunately, it's also the least severe and least progressive. Unfortunately, it's inherited, and there's a fifty-fifty chance of passing it on to offspring.

As if that weren't enough, my mother learned just a few weeks later that she had early-onset dementia.

I wasn't the only one taking a detour, it seemed. Our whole family was along for the ride, and that ride was about to get even rougher.

CHAPTER 6:

FINDING MY NICHE

Life is 10% what happens to me and 90% how I react to it.

—Charles Swindoll

n March of 2005, I began a vigorous two-month training program for my new job at the pharmaceutical company and was very excited about the opportunity. I had been learning so much about what it meant to be sick and to endure test after test, take endless medications, and never know what's coming next that I felt I had something to offer to others going through a similar experience. Plus, the manager who'd hired me had made a strong effort to recruit me, which was a huge boost to my confidence.

On the night before my last day of training, though, things took a turn.

I came back to the hotel that evening feeling great and went to bed fairly early. Around 2:30 a.m., I woke up to palpitations and a horrible chest pain. I was having trouble breathing, and my hands and feet were all tingly. Something was terribly wrong.

The next day, I got a call from Dr. Kluger's office.

"Rob," Danette said in a grave tone. "I'm afraid I've got some bad news."

I took a deep breath. "Okay, hit me with it."

"Your device has been recalled."

I knew there had been a lot of news in the papers about recalls from the major device companies, but I hadn't thought it would affect me. It was like one of those things you think happens to other people—but with that call, I was startled out of my state of denial.

"And that means," Danette continued, pulling me away from the chatter in my head, "that we need to do a software upgrade."

Yes, thanks to modern technology, they didn't even need to cut into me to fix it. All it took was a software upgrade and I would be as good as new.

My heart wasn't killing me after all!

In the months that followed, I focused my energies on another matter of the heart. After a series of less-than-exciting dates, I met a woman I really liked through an online dating service and was instantly attracted to her.

Diana was short, with shoulder-length, reddish-brown hair and a natural beauty that matched her personality. She rarely swore and didn't date around, but she was hardly naive. She had a raw, innate intelligence that wowed me, and her career as a homecare nurse seemed like a perfect fit for me, given how much time I was coming to spend in the medical system. Her caring, patient personality was exactly what I needed as I struggled to deal with my own issues, and I also fell in love with her oversized cat, Riley, and her Australian shepherd, Luna.

I had sunk into a dark depression during my transition with the new job and move back to Connecticut, but once I met Diana, the depression just began to magically dissolve. I felt I'd finally found the woman of my dreams.

The same went for my new job—or at least I thought it did. I was quickly finding that I was really good at pharmaceutical sales. I soon got glowing reviews and increased responsibility as I met and exceeded my reach and frequency quotas week after week. My new manager, Julia, was especially encouraging at first, helping me to move up the ladder.

"Rob," she said to me one day while she was joining me on my sales calls, "I've got some good news."

Julia was a strong woman, shaped like a linebacker and with twice the energy. She had short, dark hair and polished her nails with dark-red polish that perfectly matched her blood-colored lipstick. To top it all off, she wore her eyeliner thick and dark, like a stripe of black tar swiped across her eyelids. She wasn't a woman to be messed with; she was a woman who got things done.

"Good news?" I asked, brightening.

"You're doing very well," she said with a broad smile on her face. "You've done an amazing job since you've come here, and you've clearly got leadership qualities. You're on the fast track for success and I can really see you going places. Now, let's discuss your future with the company."

The conversation that followed filled my head with ideas and my heart with confidence. "Fast track" meant that Julia believed in me and was on my side.

Despite Julia's certainty in me, however, I wasn't entirely certain about the job myself. Several changes took place in the first couple months, including management changes and two territory changes, which made it difficult for me to develop a routine. The company was putting enormous pressure on representatives to sell medications, and it seemed the health of patients was not its first priority.

I also saw how self-serving the doctors could be.

One time, after I had been waiting for half an hour to meet with an exceptionally difficult doctor, a couple of really beautiful women from a rival pharmaceutical company came by. When the doctor stepped out of his office, he looked right past me and ushered them in. They were selling Viagra and I was selling a cholesterol-lowering medication. I couldn't compete with their sex appeal. And that was an experience I kept encountering: what we were selling was never as important as what perks we had to offer. Soon I realized that the job I was supposedly so good at might not be a job that was good for me.

By the end of summer, my health was deteriorating once again. I was waking up tired every morning, and by noon was totally worn out. I began having more blackouts, which meant my heart wasn't working properly again. My legs grew tired easily when I ran, and I also began to wonder if I had carpal tunnel: my fingers, wrists, and arms became sore whenever I typed and they often tingled. My hands and feet were also turning purple and getting very cold on a regular basis.

I called Dr. Ferraro, who persuaded me to go in for a stress test and an echocardiogram.

The stress test didn't go as well as I'd hoped. I could only go thirteen and a half minutes on the treadmill before wearing out—only five seconds longer than the test I'd taken shortly after having the pacemaker and defibrillator implanted.

Interestingly, the results of the echocardiogram showed that my heart had shrunk to a more normal size. Before, due to an abnormal thickening of my heart's walls—a condition called hypertrophic cardiomyopathy—my heart wall had been fifteen millimeters thick. Now it was back to twelve millimeters. Dr. Ferraro couldn't explain what was going on or why, but at least it was a good sign. As for the stiffness and weakness in my legs, she thought it could be a side effect of my heart condition or the combination of drugs I was taking.

"Don't worry," she said, "we just need to pay close attention to it and see if it gets better before making any more changes in your meds. Once I talk to Dr. Kluger, we'll get back to you on how to move forward from here."

I was relieved to think that my weak energy and limbs were probably just side effects of the meds. Those could always be adjusted—though, frankly, I was getting tired of all the different medications. Each one came with its own set of side effects, and they all interacted differently with each other. Just like the commercials that say, "Common side effects could include . . ." I had many to beware of—blurred vision, cold hands, diarrhea, dizziness, fatigue, headache, sweating, and weakness, for example. Some less frequent reactions could also include shortness of breath, trouble sleeping, loss of sex drive, and depression. To combat all those side effects, I'd have to break into a drugstore for extra supplies of Advil, Ambien, Pepto, Viagra, and Zoloft.

Dr. Ferraro and I also discussed the possibility that the symptoms might be due to the fact that Dr. Kluger's staff had adjusted the rate response of my pacemaker to speed my heart up at times. You see, the heart pumps oxygenated blood throughout the body. If your heart rate is too slow, the oxygenated blood doesn't get delivered properly and your muscles can get fatigued and fail to recover as quickly and easily as they normally would. Adjusting the rate response would automatically program the pacemaker to speed up my heart if the sensor detected an increased movement with my body.

However, having the adjustments only caused more problems. My pacemaker was now supersensitive. Just my running a couple steps to catch an elevator or standing up to cheer at a ball game would set off the device and cause my heart to beat faster, which created an extremely uncomfortable sensation.

After weeks of adjustments, we realized the rate response changes were doing more harm than good. We recognized there was something besides my heart rate that was contributing to the weakness and discomfort in my legs.

▲▲ ▲▲ ▲▲

Meanwhile, back in Chicago, my parents were still struggling with their own health problems. My mom's ongoing battle with cardiac and lung disease had continued to worsen, and ever since his muscular dystrophy diagnosis, my dad had been losing his physical mobility at an increasing pace. When he wasn't working, he stayed at home, playing solitaire on the computer or watching TV.

"You know, Dad," I said to him one day when I was visiting, "I've been thinking, and there just may be a connection between some of my health problems and your muscular dystrophy. Maybe I've inherited it too."

"Maybe," he said. He didn't like to open up about our health issues much.

"Don't forget," I added, "our hearts are like muscles, and there's a fifty-fifty chance of passing muscular dystrophy on to offspring, so I think I should talk to my doctors about that."

The next time I saw Dr. Ferraro, I mentioned my concerns. After concluding that my slow heart rate was not directly responsible for what was happening, she referred me to see a neurologist who was a leading figure with the Muscular Dystrophy Association. The doctor did some testing and told me that my arm problems were not the result of carpal tunnel, and that he suspected they were part of a neuromuscular problem.

"This is very interesting, very interesting indeed," he told me, looking over my chart. "I haven't seen any patients presenting like you, not at your age and in your physical shape. Typically, what we'd expect to see is an older patient or a younger one in a much weaker state. If you do have muscular dystrophy," he said with almost a smile on his face, "then it's a very rare form, perhaps even an undiscovered strain."

His eyebrows shot up at that last line, and his excitement was barely contained. I even felt some of it rub off on me, the way he was talking. If I did have muscular dystrophy, then I was some sort of very special case. For some reason, that thought made me feel good; maybe I could help others, I reasoned, if I helped to discover a new disease.

▲▲ ▲▲ ▲▲

I was scheduled for a battery of tests over the course of the next few weeks that would require taking more time off work. I knew I'd have to give Julia a heads-up to let her know the reason why. As I'd learned from my last job, being open and honest is always the best way to go. I had no doubt I'd get the same support from Julia and my colleagues I'd gotten at my old job once they knew what was going on, especially since it was one of the things I'd mentioned being passionate about when I was hired—that my own heart problems made me want to work with medicines that could help fight heart disease. I figured it was good timing, too. Just the week before, I had received a letter from Julia assuring me of a pending promotion.

I approached Julia prior to the start of one of our monthly meetings.

"Can I talk to you?" I asked.

"Sure, Rob," she said, greeting me with a smile. "What's up?"

"I just wanted to talk to you for a minute about why I've missed a couple of days of work, that's all."

Her smile faded, and curiosity and concern took its place. "What is it, Rob? Is there a problem?"

"Oh, it's probably nothing, I hope," I said, stammering a bit as I searched for the right words. "Just something I wanted to share with you, but can I ask that you keep it in confidence? Just between you and me?"

"Of course," she said, her eyebrows raised. "What's wrong, Rob, are you okay?"

"Well, yes and no," I said. "I mean, I'm okay as far as work is concerned, but there are some health concerns my physicians and I are looking into that require taking some time off every once in a while for appointments and testing."

"Oh my goodness!" she said, clearly concerned. "Is it serious?"

"We have no idea," I explained, trying to ease her worries that it might affect my work. "You know I have a defibrillator/pacemaker," I clarified, "and my father was recently diagnosed with muscular dystrophy. So I need to go through some additional testing because there's a chance I may have it."

"Oh, Rob, I'm so sorry to hear that," Julia said.

Before she could say anything more, I gave her the background of my health issues and assured her that despite all the flaws in my body, I put my job first and she had no reason to worry about me getting behind.

"Really, all it means is once in a while I'll have to go to a doctor's appointment or occasionally get some testing," I said. "Tomorrow I have to see a neurologist, but I'll be sure to make my sales calls, don't worry."

"Oh, don't worry about that," she said. "The important thing is that you get better and take care of yourself."

With that, I finished my work for the week and headed back to Hartford for more tests, confident that I had done the right thing.

I came to find out otherwise when I'd returned to the office the following week. After various representatives called and emailed me to ask if I was okay, it became clear that other sales associates knew about my deteriorating health and time off work. My personal information was violated, my trust betrayed. Julia was not the person I thought she was.

CHAPTER 7:

THINGS FALL APART

Success is not final, failure is not fatal: it is the courage to continue that counts.

—Winston Churchill

In the weeks that followed my return from Hartford, I grew increasingly depressed and had terrible anxiety. No matter how hard I worked or how strong my sales were, nothing I accomplished was recognized. I had no idea what I had done or said to change Julia's views of me, but I was clearly no longer on her list of favorite employees. She'd grown close to my sales partner, who had suddenly distanced herself from me as well. Where once Julia had greeted me with a big smile or given me a bit of praise for a job well done when we crossed paths, now it seemed she was monitoring my every move. Virtually overnight, it was if I'd become as welcome as a cold sore.

Despite my efforts to work harder to turn things around, I eventually had to accept that it wasn't getting any better. My sales figures were great, but I was criticized for not pushing even further ahead. Even though the only time I missed work was for doctor's appointments and I never got behind in my production goals, I was criticized for my absenteeism. Clearly, Julia wanted me out.

All this on top of my parents' deteriorating health and the possibility that I might have muscular dystrophy; I was feeling like my whole life was a constant struggle. And I was having a really hard time dealing with the uncertainty. I kept thinking that if I could somehow get my head wrapped around it all, things would calm down, but I couldn't seem to get to that place.

Instead, I settled into a dark and anxious mood where I no longer slept through the night and lived in constant fear of getting fired for the slightest mistake. If I expressed an opinion in a meeting, I was being hostile. If another worker dropped the ball, somehow I was responsible. Whatever it was or whoever did it, as far as Julia was concerned, it was my fault.

I felt like I was losing my mind.

▲▲ ▲▲ ▲▲

"I think you should consider taking some time off of work," Dr. Ferraro suggested during one of my checkups.

"Take time off?" I questioned. "I can't afford to take any time off; they'll fire me."

"You're going through a lot," she explained. "Anyone going through this kind of stress along with pressure from work needs a break. It's not healthy, and I'm concerned about your heart with so much stress."

She was right. Between work, my parents' health, and my own health worries, I was enduring more stress than I could handle. It was really taking a toll on me. I agreed to discuss it with my therapist, whom I had started seeing in recent months to help me cope with all that was going on.

▲▲ ▲▲ ▲▲

When I told my therapist about Dr. Ferraro's suggestion that I take a break from work, she immediately agreed it was something I needed to do.

"You're clearly under extreme stress, and it's going to jeopardize your physical and emotional health. I'm going to recommend that you take a disability leave."

"Disability? But I'm not disabled," I protested.

"You have a major depressive disorder and job-related anxiety with everything you are going through. You've been paying for disability insurance ever since you started working, and that's what it's there for. Just take some time off to relax. That should give you time to focus on your family and your health."

"Are you sure that's the right thing to do? What if they fire me?"

"They can't fire you. It's against the law to fire someone for taking disability leave. But that's not your worry. Right now your number one concern is your health. Take care of it."

When I got home that evening, I discussed it with Diana, and she also felt I should take the time off, even if it cost me my job.

"You need to do what's best for you," she said, wrapping her arms around me with a big hug. "If that means taking time off of work, then do it. If they fire you, that's their loss. You'll find another job, one where you're treated much better."

"Okay," I said, "I'll think about it." It was the best I could do at that point. As much as I knew I needed time off of work, I hated the idea of being a quitter. When I start something, I want to finish it, and taking time off felt like giving up. Regardless, I knew they were all right: I needed less stress in my life, not more.

I went back to work and obtained the disability paperwork I needed, and Dr. Ferraro and my therapist began to fill it out. I applied for a family medical leave and disability and was quickly approved for a leave of absence. On June 6th, 2006, I officially became disabled.

▲▲ ▲▲ ▲▲

The very next day, Julia both called and sent me an email indicating I was under investigation for sales call activities and said I needed to attend a meeting about the inquiry. So much for legal protections; legal or not, they intended to fire me.

Immediately, I called my therapist, and she instructed me not to respond. This was no way to start my recovery.

I would spend the summer reading through one allegation after another, all designed with one aim in mind: to paint me as unfit for my job and, indeed, unfit for basic human kindness. What I'd hoped would be my summer of recovery threatened to become my summer of hell.

Still, despite having to contend with the investigation against me, being away from my job helped immensely. I started exercising and eating healthier foods, and I soon felt better than I had in months.

By August, I was wondering if I'd ever find out what was wrong with me. Then a nurse from the neurology office called.

"All right," she said, "we've got your test results back."

"Okay," I said, taking a deep breath and preparing for the worst. "Hit me with it."

"We'd like to set up an appointment for next week," she said.

Next week? She knew the answer to whether or not I had muscular dystrophy right in front of her but she wasn't going to tell me for another week?

"Please, could you just tell me whether I have it or not," I pleaded. "Either way, I'll come in next week, but I can't spend the entire weekend worrying."

"I can't disclose that information over the phone," she said.

But I was relentless and would not take no for an answer.

"All right," she finally said with a heavy sigh. "I'll talk to the doctor and see what he says."

A few hours later, my neurologist called back. I could tell from the tone in his voice he wasn't happy to make the call.

"This is not how we usually handle these things," he said, sounding irritated. "Your test came back positive."

"Positive?" I asked. I wasn't sure if that was good or bad. Normally, positive is a good thing, but it sure didn't feel that way.

"It means you tested positive for myotonic dystrophy type 2, a rare form of muscular dystrophy. That's all I'm going to tell you over the phone. I'll see you next week. Good-bye."

With that, he hung up.

I sat still, dazed, staring straight ahead as I let the diagnosis register. I did have muscular dystrophy. My muscles were wasting away, just like my dad's, and there was nothing I could do to stop it.

Diana came with me to the appointment the following week, and we sat nervously in the waiting room, silent, as I was consumed with my thoughts. *Is it going to progress quickly? What will the treatment entail? Is that the reason the biopsy of my heart was full of scar tissue? Will I have to take even more medication that will probably have even more side effects? What kind of physical therapy will I have to go through? How soon before I'm in a wheelchair? What about my life expectancy?*

Diana held my hand and I did my best to calm her, as she was visibly upset and worried about the appointment. Though I was scared on the inside, I acted as if it was no big deal and I could handle it. The truth was, somehow the muscular dystrophy diagnosis was even scarier than being told I needed a defibrillator. I knew muscular dystrophy was progressive, and I knew there was no cure. I felt as if my entire future had turned black, so I hung on to those few minutes in the waiting room as perhaps my last peaceful moments before the dreaded truth of what I was facing would be presented to me. Once the doctor told me what was in store, there would be no more uncertainty, no more hope. At least sitting there in the waiting room, I could still cling to hope.

"Well, Rob," he said once we were seated in the exam room, "it looks like I was wrong."

For a brief instant, I was thrilled. He was wrong! I didn't have muscular dystrophy!

"When you first told me about your dad's diagnosis and asked me to test for it, I thought it would be a waste of time. I thought we were onto something new, something we hadn't seen before. But you were right. You've got the same thing your dad has, DM2. I must say, I was surprised."

His words grew distant as my own thoughts began to take over. Was he disappointed that I wasn't some sort of ticket to medical fame for him?

As he rambled on, his tone was so flat it sounded like he was telling me what was wrong with my car rather than my body. He was far different from the other wonderful physicians I'd been working with, all of whom really seemed to care about me. I was astounded at the sharp turn he had taken—from initially being very concerned about my case to totally bored by it.

"So what can we expect?" Diana asked, her voice nearly cracking as she held back her tears. "How soon before he starts losing muscle control?"

She was shaking she was so nervous, so I held her hand to calm her. She was even more upset than I was to receive this news.

Strangely, the words I'd just heard hadn't frightened me. Instead, I grew terribly calm; it was like my mind had decided I had to be as clear and strong as possible so I could understand what was happening. Did I have months? Or years? What would go first? My legs? My arms? My speech? I had done enough research by now to know those questions couldn't be answered; the progression is always unknown and differs from person to person; still, it was hard not to ask.

"Oh, you never can tell with these sorts of things," he answered Diana. "DM2 usually has a slow progression, so he should be fine for a while."

Still, there were questions I wanted answered. "Should I stop playing sports?" I asked. "Should I stop working out?"

I knew from studying my dad's diagnosis that there were two schools of thought about having a muscle disease. The first is that your body is like a battery and you only have so much juice before it runs out. If that's the case, then you don't want to use it up on things like working out or sports—or, in other words, having fun.

The second school of thought is that you should do whatever you can for as long as you can so you can look and feel as healthy as possible until the disease takes over. That was going to be the school of thought I'd subscribe to, but I wanted to hear the doctor's thoughts.

Instead of giving me actual answers, however, he mumbled some meaningless strings of words to the effect of he didn't know squat and I had to make my own decisions.

Then, as if that was all I needed to know, he ended our meeting and told me to check back in with him in another year.

I didn't even realize what had happened until we had left his office and were heading out to the car. He had told me nothing. Absolutely nothing.

"Check back in another year?" I said to Diana, completely confused.

"What the hell does that mean? Am I supposed to just wait around and see what happens?"

"I know, Rob," Diana said, anger and frustration taking the place of her sadness. "He was a jerk. But I'll ask around at work and we'll find out all we can."

Despite how difficult it was to learn I had myotonic muscular dystrophy type two, I was largely at peace with the diagnosis. After years of not knowing why my legs were so weak and not being able to explain my increasing fatigue and soreness, I no longer had to wonder what was wrong. I finally knew the reason and could focus my attention on how to make my life better.

Once I'd reached the point of accepting that I had muscular dystrophy, I set out to learn as much as I could about it. I got involved with the Muscular Dystrophy Association and was online every night, reaching out to other people who had muscular dystrophy. I found through the online communities far more support than I'd found from the neurologist who'd diagnosed me. Soon, one thing became clear: whether the disease progressed fast or slow, it was definitely going to progress.

Another thing that was progressing? The pharmaceutical company's determination to be rid of me. While I had never slacked off, had always met my sales goals, and had a stellar record before telling Julia about my health, they ultimately concluded that I was not a good fit. They even suggested there had to be something erroneous about the reports for my sales to be as high as they were, given the time I'd taken off work for my health issues.

When my physicians cleared me to return to work in a part-time capacity, it didn't matter. The pharmaceutical company insisted I work full time or not at all, and since my physicians wouldn't clear me for full-time work, I had to apply for long-term disability.

That became the start of yet another battle—one that went on for over a year. It was against the law to punish someone for taking a disability leave, and I could see no other reason for the company's abrupt shift from being so supportive of me to being so determined to be rid of me.

I wasn't about to go down without a fight.

I met with an attorney, and it quickly became clear that, legal or illegal, fighting an employer never turns out well. I knew my tenure at the company was over. After some stressful and ugly negotiations, I resigned. I began another job search, but now that I had been diagnosed with progressive muscle disease on top of my heart ailments, finding work was the least of my worries.

CHAPTER 8:

NO PLACE LIKE HOME

We must accept finite disappointment, but never lose infinite hope.

—Martin Luther King Jr.

It's funny how life works—how something that seems so important one minute ends up being so insignificant the next.

Diana and I were having a huge fight over something so petty. Moments after she stormed out the door, Chris called with devastating news.

"Hey, sis, what's up?" I asked, half worried that something had happened to Dad and half still stuck in the fight I'd just had with Diana.

"Robby, Mom had a stroke," she answered through tears, "and it's not good. She isn't likely to survive the night."

My mom had struggled with health problems for years. She had heart failure and also had a pacemaker. She'd smoked three packs a day ever since she was a teenager, and had severe chronic obstructive pulmonary disease as a result. Her doctors had warned her it would kill her, but she'd just ignored their cautions.

We had been worried about Mom's health for years, but she was the family caretaker and we'd just assumed she'd always be there. Now I was facing the reality that she wouldn't.

Mom had been sitting at the kitchen table, watching *Dancing with the Stars*, when the stroke occurred. She and some of her friends made a game of it. They each would watch the show and rate the dances separately, then get together for breakfast the following morning and compare their votes to those cast by the judges from the show. That's what she was doing—just sitting at the kitchen table, watching her show—when suddenly she fell out of the chair and crashed face first onto the floor.

My dad was playing solitaire on his computer in the other room when he heard the thud. By that point, he was walking with a cane and had trouble getting around, but he got up and headed to the kitchen, where he saw her on the floor. He managed to get down on his knees to help her but then realized he had to call 911. Unable to get back to his feet, he crawled across the floor to reach the phone, called for an ambulance, and then crawled back across the floor to be with her. I couldn't imagine what it must have been like for him to be so powerless.

As soon as I hung up with Chris, I called Diana, who turned right around; our huge fight was nothing but an afterthought. With my mother dying, all that mattered was getting to her side, and Diana was right there with me, helping me do that.

The first flight I could get was not until the following morning. I was convinced my mom would be dead by the time I got home, and I felt completely helpless.

▲▲ ▲▲ ▲▲

When I boarded my flight the next morning, Mom was still hanging on. I started writing her eulogy in the air, just as I had done for Rusty. It helped me to prepare myself for the fact that she wasn't going to make it. I was heartbroken to think that, just as with my brother, I wouldn't be there when she died.

When I landed at Chicago Midway International Airport, my dad was there waiting for me. I had no idea what to say—it didn't seem right to ask if Mom had died—so I just let the look on my face ask the question.

"She's still alive," he said, his voice shaking, "but it's not good. I think she's just been hanging on till you got here. They say she won't make it through the day."

We drove directly to the hospital. It was a tense, silent drive. When we got there, both my sisters were sitting with our mom, who was tethered to a lacework of tubing and wires. She was on a ventilator, unconscious, and completely unresponsive. After giving her a kiss and telling her I loved her, I stepped out of the room with my dad and sisters to discuss the options.

"She won't survive the day," Chris said. "The doctors are pretty certain this is the end."

"Not necessarily," my dad said. "I told them to do whatever they can to keep her alive."

"Dad," Chris said, "Mom's got advanced directives. She doesn't want to be kept alive if she's in this condition. We aren't respecting her wishes if we keep her alive."

The conversation became heated as Cindy, an attorney, and Chris, a nurse, bickered about whether we should let our mom pass naturally or do whatever we could to help her recover. Meanwhile, my dad retreated into his own pain, preparing for the loss of the woman he'd been married to for most of his life.

Consulting the physicians didn't help much. At first, we were told in no uncertain terms that she wouldn't make it through the night. The following morning, we were told she wouldn't make it through the day. When she did, we were told she wouldn't make it through the weekend. By the following Monday, they told us they didn't know how Mom had held on so long, but we should expect her to pass any day.

About two weeks later, Mom regained consciousness and was able to open her eyes and move her fingers. She still couldn't speak, however, and it was hard to say if she recognized any of us. Watching my mother in such a state was incomprehensibly confusing. I so badly wanted her to recover, and at the same time I so badly wanted to let her go so she wouldn't suffer any longer.

Against all odds, Mom progressively got better as time went on, and after she'd spent about two months in rehab at the hospital, a social worker met with us to discuss her care.

We all sat down expecting a discussion of the next stage of Mom's treatment, but instead the social worker told us we'd have to make arrangements for her release from the hospital by week's end.

"How can you release her?" Cindy demanded. "She can't function."

"I know it's difficult," the social worker said, her tone compassionate but firm. "But here's a list of 24-hour care agencies. Look into these options and I'm sure you'll find something that will work out."

We stared at the piece of paper, totally shocked and confused. It was just a list—no recommendations, no descriptions, only names and numbers. Despite our pleas to help us select an appropriate care facility, the social worker was unable to provide any feedback on the various agencies. That wasn't her job. Her job was to hand us a piece of paper and tell us to take our mother away.

Chris and I took the lead and agreed to interview different home care agencies. After days of phone calls, we learned that there are essentially two types of agencies: the small mom-and-pop places with Eastern European or Asian workers who speak little English, which cost about $125 a day, and the larger agencies with skilled workers, which charge up to $350 a day.

We arranged for a caregiver from one of the smaller agencies to live with my parents. It proved disastrous. My father resented having a stranger around the house—and, worse, this was a stranger who was making decisions within the home and about his and my mom's care. We ended up going through several caregivers over the course of a few months.

Fortunately, because I was on disability, I had a lot of free time to stay in Chicago with my family, and Diana often would fly back with me to lend support.

As time passed, our mom was able to recognize people again, but she had a lot of trouble speaking; sometimes we could sort of understand what she was trying to say, but often we couldn't. Over time, she also regained her ability to walk a bit, but she never fully recovered. A year after her stroke, we had to put her in an assisted living facility, leaving my dad on his own. Though he had his struggles with mobility, he could take care of himself without a caregiver.

With all the problems my family was facing, it became increasingly clear that I couldn't continue to live in Connecticut, that I would need to move back to Chicago to help my family. Life was striking our family hard, and we had to stick together.

I began looking for work in Chicago but was apprehensive. My experience with the pharmaceutical company and the cruel way Julia had turned on me had left me nervous about experiencing a repeat scenario with another company. My health was good on a day-to-day basis, but I had two serious, progressive diseases that would require medical treatment and testing for the rest of my life. Would another employer even want me?

Fortunately, the place where I landed was an ideal match. Advocate Health Care was in the process of creating a new job within hospice care, and it fit great with where I was and what I wanted to do. They felt the same way about me and offered me the job.

Meanwhile, Diana and I needed to have a serious talk about our future. She had never lived anywhere but the small town in Connecticut where she'd grown up, and even though she loved Chicago, it seemed like a world away to her. Still, we were in love, so she decided to take the risk, quit her job in Connecticut, and moved with me to the Windy City—which, unbeknownst to many, was given that name for the city's hot-air-blowing politicians, not the windy conditions.

By that point I was thirty-three years old and felt it was time to settle down. I bought a townhouse with some money I'd saved up—Diana helped me pick it out—and started my new career.

The job was wonderful. I was responsible for educating health-care professionals about the benefits of hospice and end-of-life care within a territory I'd been assigned. I also tried to help doctors identify the right level of care for patients. What I had discovered in my research was that a lot of times people aren't referred to hospice care until the bitter end, even though hospice is available for people with a life expectancy of six months or less, and many people with those diagnoses live much longer. In other words, most families weren't getting the help they had a right to receive. Also, many families believe that turning to hospice care is giving up, when it's really about making the patient more comfortable.

It was my job to clear up those misconceptions for health professionals and families—to help them understand that the patients would be fighting just as hard but simply changing their focus to relieve unnecessary physical, emotional, and spiritual suffering, and to make every day count.

I didn't feel like a salesperson when I talked to healthcare professionals and families about hospice care. I had lost my brother after years of health issues and mental illness, watched my father decline month after month from muscular dystrophy, and seen my mother unable to care for herself after experiencing a stroke. I was also very aware of my own mortality and knew that some level of immobility awaited me in my future. I was speaking from the heart about a real problem in our society that I wanted to help address. That was a job I could believe in.

Best of all, my employers knew about my heart problems from the start, so instead of viewing me as a problem, they viewed me as a solution—someone worth investing in.

Back at home, though, it was a different story altogether.

With Diana's help in picking out the furniture, paint colors, plants, and other decorations, the townhome was becoming cozier every day, yet the vibe was getting icy.

"Yeah, I've fixed it up," she'd reply when I'd point out how nice the townhouse had become. "But it's not my house; it's yours."

I was so focused on my new job and being close to family again that I hadn't given much thought to how Diana must be feeling, or giving her the attention she deserved. She was in a rut—similar to the one she'd helped me through when I first moved to Connecticut—and I wasn't doing nearly as much as I could and should to help her with the transition.

Soon, Diana became depressed and was no longer the happy, active girl I had met less than two years before. She would go from sad to mad, and then the fights would start.

"I didn't think it would be so hard to adjust here," she kept saying. "I have no friends, no job, no nothing."

At the time, I didn't want to hear it. I just wanted her to be happy and stop complaining. So, instead of helping her to feel more secure in our home, I got defensive.

"Here we go again," I'd say. "No matter what I say or do, it's still not enough."

After constant bickering, we began seeing a therapist, but all we ended up doing was blaming each other for our problems.

One thing I have learned over time is that we create our own realities. In this situation, after having decided that Diana was the one with the problem, I didn't examine my own behavior or consider how it was negatively impacting the relationship. In hindsight, however, I realize it was my fault—that I was blinded to how badly I was botching the love I'd been seeking all my life.

Trying to avoid the situation, I'd stay away from home as much as I could and just put all my energies into my job and my family, areas of my life where I now felt both respected and appreciated. As long as I had my family, my home, and my job, I thought, I would be okay—with or without Diana in my life.

Unsurprisingly, our relationship imploded in no time. By the spring of 2008, a year after we'd moved to Chicago, the woman I so deeply loved had decided she'd had enough. She was moving back to Connecticut.

▲▲　▲▲　▲▲

On the very same day Diana and I said our good-byes and she drove back to Connecticut, I was delivered another blow: at age sixty-four, my dad was diagnosed with Stage IV throat cancer. He needed a laryngectomy, in which he'd have his larynx removed and a hole punched through his throat so he could breathe.

After the surgery, my dad not only had to learn an entirely new way to swallow, he also lost his ability to speak and fell into a world of silence. He became very irritable and showed all his emotional frustration in his facial expressions, pointing at things and acting like he was yelling, though no words were coming out.

It was heartbreaking to witness. My dad always had been a tough guy, the kind of guy who never complained of pain and never let anyone see him vulnerable. Now, muscular dystrophy and cancer had knocked him down with one punch after another. It didn't help to think that it only would be a matter of time before I suffered some of the same blows.

For years as a kid, I had to wear a patch over my good right eye in order to strengthen the muscle stigmatism (lazy eye) in my left eye. Peter Pan, beware: the unfortunate look earned me the nickname "Captain Hook."

By the time I reached high school, football had become my escape and was a way for me to release my built-up anger and frustration. This picture is from my senior year in 1991, just days before I was told my broken back would put an end to my career and college scholarship offers.

*For years, my mom would take my siblings and me for professional portraits.
Here we are in 1992, the last group picture before my brother died in 2004.
From left are my sister Cindy, brother Rusty, sister Chris, and myself.*

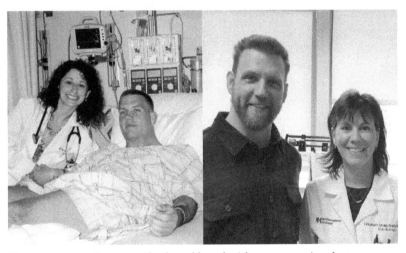

*Throughout my diagnoses, I've been blessed with some amazing doctors.
Among them are Dr. Melissa Ferarro-Borgida (left), who was my primary
cardiologist from 2003–2007, and Dr. Elizabeth McNally (right), who is an
expert in cardiovascular disease and evaluation, including muscular dystrophy
and cardiomyopathy.*

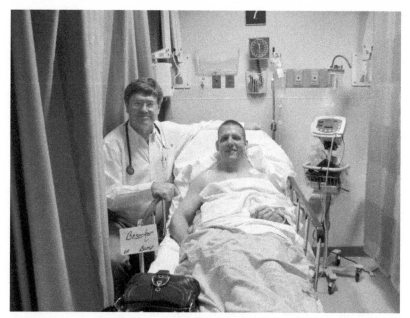

Since I moved back to Chicago in 2007, Dr. Thomas Bump has been my primary cardiologist, as well as my biggest supporter and advocate. Here, he poses with me just before performing my defibrillator replacement surgery in 2008.

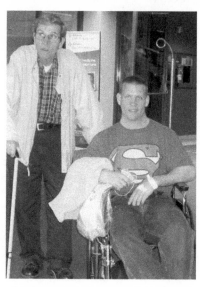

Though my father and I almost never expressed our love for one another verbally, we were always there for each other. Here, my dad is walking with me after my defibrillator replacement surgery in 2008, the day before he was diagnosed with stage IV throat cancer.

Watching my father decline so rapidly with deteriorating muscle disease made me question my own future with the same diagnosis. I began a journey to pursue as many of my goals as I could while I was still able. Here I am in 2008 on the Great Wall of China, months before my father lost his battle with terminal cancer.

It was while traveling to Antarctica, my seventh and final continent, when I had the good fortune of meeting Peter Hillary (left)—son of Sir Edmund Hillary, who was the first to summit Mount Everest—and Mervyn English (right), Hillary's climbing partner and friend. Hearing Hillary's stories about climbing planted the seed for my own future adventure.

Upon my release from my second surgery and hospital stay in 2011 to replace my defective defibrillator and leads, my first stop was to see my mom at her assisted living facility. Though she lost the ability to use her right arm after a massive stroke in 2006, she never lost her beautiful smile.

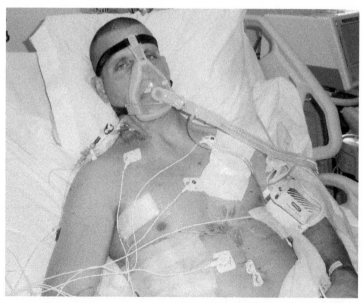

Here I am recovering from my fifth and final cardiac procedure in November 2011, when doctors gained access to my heart through openings in my chest, groin, and neck while inserting breathing tubes on both sides of my chest.

It's amazing how quickly things can change. In 2010, I was enjoying a lovely trip to Hawaii with friends. Only one year later, I was recovering from my fifth cardiac procedure, a hybrid mini-maze procedure to correct my rapid cardiac rhythms.

The Muscular Dystrophy Association (MDA) has been an important part of my life since my father and I were diagnosed with myotonic muscular dystrophy type 2 in 2005–2006. Not only am I able to share my strength with others, I also gain a valuable perspective on life from some of the amazing clients and families I meet. Here I am at the 2015 Chicago Marathon with Cameron and Reagan, where we cheered on runners and supporters of the MDA.

PART II

CHAPTER 9:

CHANGE IS GOOD

God grant me the serenity to accept the things I cannot change, the courage to change the things I can, and the wisdom to know the difference.

—The Serenity Prayer by Reinhold Niebuhr

Seeing my parents' health decline, as well as watching so many lives come to an end through my work in hospice care, compelled me to look inward. As I grappled with my own mortality and what physical limitations might result from my muscular dystrophy, I began to consider what I wanted to accomplish in life. One thing I knew I wanted was to see as much of the world as I could while I still was able to walk.

By that point, I already had traveled to Europe, South America, Australia, and Africa, and there were only two continents I had never been to: Asia and Antarctica. I was determined to see them both before my health conditions prevented it.

Diana and I had gone to Egypt to see the great pyramids. Gazing at those man-made wonders, I had been stunned not only by the Egyptians' will and tenacity to erect what were the tallest structures in the world for thousands of years but also by the fact that these monuments have survived all this time, rising from the sands as a testament to human endurance. I wanted to see more man-made wonders—I wanted to see the Great Wall of China.

I invited Chris, who also enjoys traveling, to join me on the trip. First, we'd fly to China and see Beijing and the Great Wall, then we'd embark on a cruise that would take us through much of Southeast Asia.

I was mesmerized by the Great Wall. It was utterly beautiful, curving through the mountains like a ribbon of stone. As our tour group approached the Badaling entrance, which was the finishing point of the 2008 Summer Olympics Urban Road Cycling Course, I couldn't wait to reach it and hurried ahead. I walked as fast as I could, and then I broke into a jog, and then, finally, I ran straight for the nearest steps to take me to the top.

I felt like I was in a race—a race against my own mortality, a race against the DM2 I knew could one day cripple me. Whether that meant my future would be in a wheelchair like my grandpa or leaning on a cane like my father, I didn't know, but the day would probably come when I couldn't ascend those stairs. I didn't know when or how that day would come, or if my heart would strike me down beforehand, but I knew one thing: that day had not yet arrived. I could still walk, I could still talk, and on a good day, I could run. And there was no doubt about it—today was a good day.

The ancient steps were worn and slick with dust—and incredibly steep. At first, I took them two at a time, anxious to reach the top, but I hadn't gone far before I realized that I had to pace myself.

When I finally stood upon the wall, I didn't know whether to turn left or right. There is a superstition that you only can go in one direction, but I wasn't about to let some old superstition limit me. I decided to explore both ways.

I turned left, toward the steepest direction, and began to jog. When I found myself too far from the group, I turned around and jogged downhill in the other direction, pausing every now and then for Chris to catch up to me.

There were many places to stop for a break, and whenever the group paused to rest I kept on going, reaching the next break area before any-one else. I savored the time alone. I felt incredibly free, incredibly strong, and incredibly blessed to be on the other side of the world and touching my feet upon such an amazing achievement. At one point I stopped, gazing along the serpentine wall that continued before me, and thought of all the people with muscular dystrophy and other disabilities who couldn't possibly be doing what I was doing.

This walk along the Wall is for them, I thought.

I also thought of all the people with muscular dystrophy and other disabilities who could still walk but would never dare travel so far, attempt something so strenuous, for fear they wouldn't make it.

This walk along the Wall is for you, too, I thought, understanding all too well how fears can limit our achievements.

Was it my fear that kept me from moving forward with Diana? I began to wonder.

Had I been so afraid that it might not work that I didn't make the extra effort to love her as she deserved to be loved? How I wished she were standing by my side and sharing this moment with me.

"Hey, Robby, isn't this amazing?"

I turned and there was Chris, a bit out of breath. I smiled.

"Yep," I agreed, wanting to keep my private thoughts private. "That's exactly what I was thinking."

After visiting the Great Wall for several hours and many other local sites over the course of three days, we embarked on a sixteen-day cruise that included stops in China, Japan, Taiwan, Vietnam, and Singapore. The trip was incredible; by the time we reached Thailand, however, Chris and I were ready to go home. We weren't enjoying our time together. The stress of caring for our parents and watching them suffer had gotten to us both, and the tension between us had increased to a point where we spent most of our time either avoiding each other or snapping at each other.

After two days of touring Bangkok, we flew home, a day earlier than most of the other passengers. The cruise line had offered two- or three-day packages in Bangkok. We had opted for the former—which turned out to be a good thing, and not just because we weren't getting along. An uprising took place right after we left, and security came down hard. Thousands of anti-government protesters stormed the airports to protest the return of Thai Prime Minister Somchai Wongsawat, who had committed electoral fraud. The People's Alliance for Democracy, which was leading the protests, said it would not end its occupation of Bangkok's airports until the prime minister resigned.

As a result, authorities had to cancel all incoming and outgoing flights. We were on what turned out to be the last plane that departed the country that day. Meanwhile, the rest of our group, and thousands of other tourists, were stranded in Thailand for up to two weeks, unable even to leave their hotels.

▲▲ ▲▲ ▲▲

By the time Chris and I returned home in early December, our father was very sick. He had already been through chemotherapy and radiation treatments, but the cancer had spread through his body and he had only weeks to live. We got him into hospice care through the company I worked for and did our best to comfort him.

The holidays that year were unsurprisingly bleak. Our mother was still struggling but hanging on, our father was dying, Diana was gone, and Chris and I still hadn't recovered from the tension that had wedged itself between us on our trip.

A month later, on January 2nd, 2009, at approximately 1:15 a.m., my father passed away.

▲▲ ▲▲ ▲▲

They say death in the family can bring people closer together, or it can rip them apart. For us, there was no question—it ripped me, Chris, and Cindy further apart.

During my dad's final days, however, I probably felt the closest to him I'd experienced in all my life. Before he lost consciousness, he told me more than once that he loved me, even hugging and holding me at times.

"I love you, too, Dad," I said, squeezing his hand gently and kissing him on the forehead. I know that he died knowing he was loved, and that's really what we all want, I've come to realize, having watched so many people die. We all just want to know we mattered.

My dad mattered.

▲▲ ▲▲ ▲▲

Two years later, it was time for another big trip. By then, Chris and I were getting along fairly well. We had gotten over the tension that had developed during our trip to Asia, and even the anger that had festered between us following my dad's death. So when I suggested a National Geographic cruise to Antarctica, she said, "Sure, why not?"

The next thing we knew, we were flying to Chile, where we stayed a few days before flying to Ushuaia, Argentina, the southernmost city in the world. There, we boarded the cruise ship that would take us through the Drake Passage to Antarctica.

The Drake Passage is one of the most turbulent passages in the world, with three oceans—the Pacific, Atlantic, and Southern—all joining to create a rough whirlpool of waves. Making matters worse, the weather was terrible, and we saw one ship that had been badly damaged while traveling through the Passage, a foreboding omen if ever there was one.

Once we were moving, we saw nothing but magnificent icebergs and infinite deep-blue water, not an island in sight. We coasted for two days and saw whales, dolphins, albatrosses, and, on the occasional ice floe, penguins. It was a fascinating voyage and hugely enjoyable—aside from the ship's violent rocking.

It was also educational. There were all kinds of lectures on the ship, and we learned that while the North Pole is actually nothing but ice and snow, Antarctica is a land mass covered in massive sheets of ice. Even more surprising, they taught us that at approximately 5.5 million square miles, it's classified as the largest desert on Earth—there is so little precipitation throughout the year that it only can support very specialized life forms.

The concept of such a bone-chilling, ice-covered landscape being a desert amazed me, and I began to reflect on all the species we'd seen so far that had evolved to live in these harsh conditions. Despite all the limitations Antarctica presented, rather than fleeing, each of the birds, fish, and fowl we were seeing had somehow survived by adapting to the environment, where darkness could last for months and the temperature could drop to almost 130 degrees below zero. Through evolution, their behaviors were altered to adapt to their environment. They learned not just to protect themselves but also each other. Their instinct to survive had kept them alive.

As my body deteriorated, that same instinct to survive was becoming stronger in me every day. As I'd prepared for the trip, I had learned after meeting with my doctors that in addition to the heart disorders and the MD, I had scoliosis in my neck, degenerative disc disease in my back, and arthritis in both. I was in a great deal of pain, but I was learning new behaviors to get through the trip—slowing my pace when I needed to, challenging myself when I could. To keep my heart rate under control, I was also learning how to govern some of my hot-tempered emotions. Ever so slowly, I was adapting to my new normal.

I have always used the Serenity Prayer as a guide and firmly believe what it says about changing what we can, accepting what we cannot, and knowing the difference between the two. However, adaptation, I was coming to realize during this trip to Antarctica, could be far more powerful than trying to change what can't be changed. I couldn't change my heart conditions, and I couldn't change the fact that I had muscular dystrophy, but I certainly could overcome my obstacles and adapt to my new life in a way that would enhance my survival.

After forty-eight hours on the ship, I was relieved when we finally dropped anchor near Deception Island, a volcanic crater at the tip of Antarctica that is used as a research station for scientists. It gets its curious name for its deceiving appearance—it looks like a normal island but actually has a narrow opening to a body of water in the middle, with the land shaped around it resembling a ring. We broke into smaller groups and each took a motor-powered Zodiac to land and do some exploring.

I was surprised it wasn't colder. It was actually warmer in Antarctica at that time than it was in Chicago—December is summertime at the bottom of the world, after all.

"Make sure you stay close to your guide and don't veer off the path," the tour guides instructed us. "And whatever you do, don't approach the penguins!"

"Yeah, right," I said to Chris in a low voice, "like I'm Batman battling the Penguin!"

"Stop it!" Chris said, smiling. "We need to pay attention."

"Penguins have no human predators, so they aren't afraid of you. They might approach you, but don't touch them. If they get within ten feet of you, they may not be afraid, but they will be nervous, and their behavior can be unpredictable. Don't back up, just stop where you are and let them check you out."

We got off the Zodiac and began hiking into the endless glacial world. There was nothing but color—the white and blue of the ice and sky, the black, brown, and gray of the surrounding rocks and hills, and all of it peppered with black-and-white penguins. The penguins were everywhere, more penguins than you'd ever want to see in your life, hobbling around like thousands of miniature Charlie Chaplins. They were gorgeous—and also disgusting. They walked in a line, following trails and pooping with every step.

"Eww!" Chris cried, covering her nose. "It really stinks!"

"Does it?" I asked. I had no idea what it smelled like; I don't know what anything smells like, for that matter. I was born without a sense of smell—a rare abnormality called anosmia. It's a great loss, I am told, but judging by the look on Chris's face, I felt blessed to be spared the smell of penguin crap.

There were times the penguins did come close, sometimes as close as five feet.

When they did, we would stop, just as the guide told us to, and watch them. Up to that point, my only experience with penguins had been at the zoo or watching *Batman* on TV.

By the end of the day, I'd seen so many penguins I was wishing we *were* at the North Pole. Still, I wouldn't have traded that day for any other. I was mesmerized.

It was fascinating because at that time of year in Antarctica, it never grew completely dark; the night was absolutely gorgeous, with the sun setting for no more than an hour or so. I had a hard time sleeping, but the experience was so breathtakingly surreal that I barely noticed how exhausted I was.

Topping off the incredible trip was an amazing speaker: Peter Hillary, son of Sir Edmund Hillary, who, along with Tenzing Norgay, was the first to reach the summit of Mount Everest on May 29th, 1953.

Peter Hillary was every bit as adventurous as his famed father and had climbed Mount Everest five times—the first time when he was only eleven years old. He had also completed the Seven Summits, reaching the top of the highest peak on each of the seven continents. If anything was more fascinating than the polar world we were cruising through, it was listening to his inspiring talks.

Hillary was a balding, animated guy who talked with his hands as much as his mouth. When he took to the stage, he instantly captivated the audience with his stories and wisdom.

"There you are," he said, talking about his love of scaling mountains, "thrown together with a bunch of mountaineers who are adventurous and ambitious and want to see if they can get to the top of the mountain. There's nothing like it. You need to rely on each other. It's teamwork."

Up until then, I had considered mountain climbing a particularly solitary sport, yet here he was talking about it like it was football or baseball—a sport made all the more exhilarating because you were working together as a team to make something happen.

"It's the uncertainty of taking on a challenge that makes it so exciting," he continued. "You don't know what you're going to encounter. You don't know what's going to happen. And not knowing is what makes it so exciting!"

He was speaking to nearly a hundred people, but as far as I was concerned he was speaking directly to me. That was exactly how I'd felt coming to Antarctica and during all of my travels. I never knew what was going to happen, and that uncertainty became my drive. I wanted to know.

It was ironic, of course, because the uncertainty of my health was what made my diagnoses all the more devastating—not knowing what would happen to me, not knowing how I'd end up. I had always viewed that uncertainty as something bad, something I wanted so desperately to control. Yet in other aspects of my life, uncertainty had fueled my passions. Could I begin to view the uncertainty of my own future in a different light?

"Sure, it's uncomfortable at times," he went on, "but discomfort turns into experiences you'll never forget. We're taught to seek comfort in life and to avoid discomfort. But discomfort is part of the experience; it helps us to remember, and it helps us to prepare."

I thought about that, and what he said rang true. I did remember the times when I'd experienced discomfort much more than I remembered the comforts. Plus, I didn't necessarily remember those times as bad experiences—I felt a sense of victory in having endured many of them.

He was also right that it helps us to prepare. After all, if I had no sense of discomfort, I wouldn't have brought warm clothes to Antarctica! I'd prepared to avoid discomfort, but the discomfort of the voyage was itself one of the most memorable aspects of the trip. It wouldn't have been half as exciting if the climate had been balmy.

"Preparation is everything," Hillary continued. "By preparing, you reduce risk. You can never eliminate risk altogether, and that's where fear comes from. We try to avoid fear, but I like fear. Fear makes you careful. Fear helps you to be prepared, and being prepared for things going wrong can help you handle them when they do."

I had been so afraid of my future, so afraid of ending up in a wheelchair, of deteriorating like my father, of losing all control. I had been afraid of the pain and suffering leading up to my own death, afraid that if the world continued without me once I died, somehow my life wouldn't have really mattered.

I had been afraid to love, having grown up in an atmosphere in which vulnerability led to hurt feelings—so much so that when I found love with Diana I had pushed her away, thinking all the while I was pushing her away because she wasn't the perfect love. But what love is perfect?

All my life, I'd lived with fear, and here was a man who had climbed the tallest peak of every continent, telling me that fear didn't keep him from having adventures, it was what motivated him to have them.

Sure, I'd heard plenty of clichés about facing our fears, but this was the first time I'd heard anyone say that fear was a good thing, that it could help me make better decisions—if I let it. If I kept viewing it as a "bad" emotion, it wouldn't serve me, it would lead me to run or hide. But if I could start thinking about fear as a teacher, as a key component to preparation, it would help me.

My thoughts were on fire listening to Peter Hillary. Then he said something that changed my entire outlook. Like the sermon about detours I'd listened to in Orlando, his words hit a chord inside me that turned my whole life around: "When you stand back," he said, "you can see the ledge you're aiming for. You can see all the features of that ledge, and you start to think about how you can get there and what it's going to be like once you get there, and you start climbing. But in all the climbs I've made, I've never reached that ledge. That's because what you see from the distance is entirely different from the place you reach. Once you're there, you see it so close up that you see it in a completely different way. The ledge you end up on is never the ledge you thought you'd reach. And that's what makes it so exciting."

After hearing Hillary speak, I was transformed. I felt like I could do anything—and I did. On December 11th, 2010, almost two years to the day after I was told my father was going to die, I took a polar plunge and jumped into the frigid waters of Antarctica.

I was really scared that I might not be able to do it because of my heart, but not only did I do it, I did it *twice*. And yeah, it sure as hell was uncomfortable. It was also an absolutely amazing experience most people in this world don't get, however, and I will never forget the thrill of plunging through that deep-blue, ice-cold Antarctic water, surrounded by penguins and seals—or how good it felt to warm up in the sauna afterwards.

Fear, I decided, would serve me. It would drive me to adventure for as long as my body would allow it.

Before I could allow my body to go on another adventure, though, there was one fear I needed to conquer. My heart condition had been getting worse again over the last year, and my doctors had recommended that I have an ablation, a serious but common procedure in which a thin wire would be guided through the femoral artery and into my heart, where electrical impulses could be sent into my heart.

"It is a serious procedure, but it's fairly common," my cardiologist had told me.

At the time I listened and nodded, but I wanted to avoid the procedure for as long as I could, to pretend it was just a bad dream and would all go away.

When I returned from Antarctica, however, I had a different response.

"Yeah," I said, "I'm going to do everything I have to do. So about that ablation? Bring it on."

CHAPTER 10:

KNOCKED BACK DOWN

It's not whether you get knocked down; it's whether you get back up.

—Vince Lombardi

I returned from Antarctica mentally ready to have the ablation, a procedure Dr. Ferraro had warned me about when we first met in 2003.

As she'd explained to me then, an ablation requires using high-energy radio frequencies to cauterize certain pieces of the heart that are beating abnormally. I had likened it to a band playing up on stage with one of the members playing out of tune and aiming a high-frequency laser at the faulty player to eliminate that member from the band.

"You mean you're going to kill parts of my heart?" I had asked Dr. Ferraro back then.

She smiled. "Only if we have to. Let's hope it doesn't come to that."

Well, it didn't come to that until 2011, when two of my cardiologists, Dr. Bump and Dr. McNally, told me it was time for an ablation. The number of irregularities with my heart rhythm kept increasing, and an ablation was the recommended course of action to fix it.

I'd had enough tests and procedures by that point that I thought of it as just another thing, no big deal. I figured if I kept a positive attitude, everything would be fine.

▲▲ ▲▲ ▲▲

On March 9, 2011, the morning of the procedure, after I had signed several documents acknowledging that I could die from whatever complications arose that day, the medical team prepped me for the big event, starting with another esophageal echocardiogram. I'd forgotten just how awful that test was—first having to drink the nasty-tasting fluid to numb my throat, which was like drinking cement, then suffering through the nurse spraying a topical anesthesia medication in my mouth and shoving a tube down my throat in order to see my heart. I felt like I was choking.

Finally, I was wheeled into the surgical unit, where the anesthesiologist knocked me out.

When I came to after the five-hour surgery, Dr. Spear, who had performed the ablation, came to my bedside.

"Hi, Rob," he said. "How're you feeling?"

"Like I just got run over by a bus, but otherwise great!" I told him, still groggy from the anesthesia. I felt like I'd been skewered through my chest and groin (the doctors had run their cardiac catheters through punctured holes in my groin all the way up to my heart for the procedure).

"I just want you to know that everything went extremely well," he said with a salesman's smile. "Textbook! You'll be back on your feet in no time."

▲▲ ▲▲ ▲▲

It was three days after the surgery, around 2:30 a.m., and I was finally getting ready for bed. Having problems sleeping is a common symptom of myotonic muscular dystrophy: My sleep patterns are inconsistent and sometimes, no matter how exhausted I am, I cannot fall asleep. Then, regardless of how much sleep I do get, I have a continuous feeling of fatigue.

Just as I was reaching my bed, my heart began to race uncontrollably. I grabbed for the stethoscope in my bedside table that I've had ever since my AFib diagnosis in 2000 and began listening to my heart. It sounded like a machine gun was going off in my chest. It was absurdly fast—what I'd later find out was more than 250 beats per minute. Hearts normally beat once per second, and here mine was, beating four times that much—it was terrifying.

Then, within seconds after checking my heart rate, *WHAM!!*—my racing heart caused the defibrillator to shock me. In all the years I'd had my device implanted, it had never gone off. And so began my night of hell.

Before that night, through all my activities and adventures, despite all my heart and health problems, I'd never had to call 911, and my defibrillator had never gone off. Now, as I write this, I've had six of these ambulance rides. One thing they have all taught me—something I didn't quite know then—is that there's not much the paramedics can do for rapid atrial heart rate. They can take your vitals, start an IV, prepare you for transport, and try to calm you down on the way to hospital, but there is no drug they can give for my condition.

"Hold your breath and bear down," the female paramedic riding with me in the back instructed. "Push as if your life depends on it; push really, really hard, to slow your heart. Clench every muscle in your body."

As I lay there listening to the siren of the ambulance racing me to the nearest hospital, my new goal became making it there alive, so I clenched, pushed, and answered all the paramedics' questions just to stay awake.

Upon our arrival at Palos Community Hospital, I was wheeled into a room in the emergency department, still wrapped like a mummy with the blankets on.

A nurse came to check on me, followed by a doctor coming in to discuss my heart history. Then the paramedics as well as the woman who checked me into the hospital were having me sign documents.

Time and time again, I discussed my heart history, the ablation from a couple days prior, and my activities of the weekend. All the while, my heart continued beating at an absurd pace. I wondered how much more discomfort I would have to endure before a doctor would help me.

More than an hour passed before the emergency room physician was able to contact a cardiologist from the practice of Drs. Bump and Spear to confirm my status and obtain permission to begin an intravenous medication called Amiodarone, a potent antiarrhythmic with potential long-term side effects. My doctors had avoided giving it to me through the years, but now, it seemed, we couldn't escape it.

"Is there anyone we can call for you?" the woman who'd checked me in asked.

"My sister Chris," I said. "She's the only one."

Chris and I hadn't talked in months after struggling again to get along during our trip to Antarctica, and she had only recently returned from her first contract on a cruise ship as a medical officer. The woman returned a short while later to let me know she had talked to Chris, who had said she wanted to receive updates by phone but would not be coming to the hospital to see me.

I tried to absorb this news and think of someone else to call so I wouldn't be alone, but I couldn't think of anyone I could bother at three in the morning. Just as I questioned my health, I began to question my relationships. Were my friends really more like friendly acquaintances?

Tears welled up my eyes. I had never felt more alone.

▲▲ ▲▲ ▲▲

A few hours later my heart rate had slowed from 250 beats a minute to 150—better, but it was still too fast and I remained exhausted and uncomfortable.

I was staring at the ceiling, my eyes open wide and my mind outpacing my heart, when out of the corner of my eye I saw someone standing at the entrance to my room. I turned my head and there, illuminated by the searing hospital lights, was Chris.

Without saying a word, she walked into the room and sat down.

"Why do you hate me?" I finally asked, breaking the silence of what felt like forever.

After a brief pause, she responded, "I don't hate you, Robby. I just don't like you sometimes. You remind me too much of your father."

She criticized my desire to control a situation and condemned the frugal nature of my spending habits.

"Why is that such a bad thing?" I asked. "And how does that affect you?"

We were both exhausted, but with the combination of her softness for the situation and my calmness in the moment, we were able to have a real conversation for the first time in months.

▲▲ ▲▲ ▲▲

Two days went by before a device representative finally came to check my ICD. We learned that the device had malfunctioned; while the defibrillator was firing, one of the wires, or leads, had cracked, so when the defibrillator went off my whole body had absorbed the shock—not just my heart. Thus, while my body was feeling all the pain, my heart wasn't getting all the treatment.

An emergency surgery was needed to change the device and to remove and replace all the leads, the wiring that was tethered to my heart through my veins. This would be my second heart procedure in less than a week.

I was transferred by another ambulance to Advocate Christ Medical Center.

Dr. Petropulos, the lead doctor of the cardiology group that included both Dr. Bump and Dr. Spear, performed this surgery. After I was cut open, he noticed the leads were attached to a very thin wall of my heart and was uncomfortable removing them—the risk of puncturing a hole in the heart during the extraction was too great. Instead, he decided to cap off the wires (rendering them useless) and install new leads, leaving me with two sets of wires in my body.

This time, when they wheeled me out after surgery, there was no doctor waiting to tell me how well everything had gone.

For years, since my original device had been implanted, I had been on blood thinners because an irregular heartbeat and abnormal pumping of the heart can cause pooling and clotting of the blood. If one of those clots breaks loose and is released in the bloodstream, it can make its way to the brain, causing a stroke.

Before the procedure, however, they'd had to take me off of the blood thinners to decrease the risk of me bleeding to death as a result of the surgery. Unfortunately, before I regained consciousness from the anesthesia used for the operation, a nurse began my medications again and included a shot of a blood thinner—a big mistake. This caused blood to pool around my incision site, forming a massive hematoma in my chest that was terribly swollen and painful.

"We're going to need to do another procedure," Dr. Spear told me while examining the problem. "We need to decrease the swelling in your chest immediately. You could be at risk of infection if it doesn't go down right away."

It was called a compression procedure: a tremendous amount of pressure was put directly over the swelling to distribute blood from the site. With most of my previous procedures, doctors had played down the pain, but for this one, Dr. Spear told me it was going to hurt like hell. It did.

I spent the next few days in the hospital, during which time quite a few friends came to see me, as did my sister Cindy and youngest niece, Becca. As had happened with Chris, the tension between me and Cindy eased as questions surrounding my health grew.

There were no answers about what had happened or why; the abnormally high atrial tachycardia was a freak incident, I was told, and all I could do was hope it wouldn't happen again.

⛰ ⛰ ⛰

Going back home at week's end, I was terrified of another recurrence happening while I was all alone. Thankfully, there were people in my life that showed up to keep me company, so I was not alone.

As a single man in my mid-thirties who didn't drink, it could be difficult to make friends. By participating in an online social networking site called Meetup, however, I had made several close acquaintances through the years. Though I hardly knew many of the members outside the group events, several stepped up and helped to support me in my time of need. One woman, Christina, organized a schedule with members of the group who knew me. Every day for the next week, someone stayed with me 24/7. I knew I couldn't have made it alone, but never in a million years would I have thought I would receive so much support from strangers. The greatest help, I learned, can come from those you least expect.

It was less than a week before blood began leaking out of the incision site in my chest and soaking through my bandage and clothes. When the bleeding wouldn't stop, Dr. Bump recommended I return to the hospital.

I waited all day in the hospital room. When day turned into evening, Dr. Bump finally stopped by to discuss two options, ranging from bad to worse.

The first was a peripherally inserted center catheter (PICC), which is essentially a long tube through which medicine can be fed directly to the heart. The downside is that it can potentially cause a life-threatening infection in the bloodstream. The second was a surgery to drain the blood from the hematoma. If an infection already had set in at the site, an emergency surgery would have to be performed to remove all the equipment in my chest.

Later, the infectious disease specialist told me the PICC line was a bad idea.

"Well, if it's such a bad idea, why was it recommended in the first place?" I asked.

"I don't know," he said.

That seemed to be the mantra of my entire diagnosis.

The next day, the problem was solved—and all it required was a simple solution. Dr. Bump realized that one of my Steri-Strips, an alternative to stitches to help close a wound from surgery, had been accidentally removed by one of the home health nurses during a visit. He applied a fresh new set to close the wound, and I was released from the hospital that afternoon.

Still, my team of physicians hadn't identified what had caused my heart to beat so out of control after the ablation, and the uncertainty of it all haunted me.

It was turning out to be one hell of a year, and spring hadn't even arrived yet.

CHAPTER 11:

THE SHOCK EFFECT

That which doesn't kill us makes us stronger.

—Friedrich Wilhelm Nietzsche

The spring of 2011 was full of doctor appointments and follow-up testing. Each visit included an interrogation of my defibrillator, which records every abnormal heart rhythm. Although the abnormal rhythms were diminishing in frequency and my heart had not raced anywhere near the speed it had the night my defibrillator fired eighteen times, I felt miserable, and my symptoms were far worse than what I'd been experiencing prior to the ablation. I remained fearful and continued to question whether I was making any progress.

"I'm scared!" I said to one of the cardiologists during a visit. "I'm worried about getting shocked again."

"Inappropriate shocks can happen," he said, exhibiting zero sensitivity to my fears. "If you were to get shocked once a year, I'm okay with that."

I was furious and deeply hurt. Although I realize inappropriate shocks may occur, his arrogant, nonchalant attitude and lack of empathy were totally unacceptable. *If only he knew what it feels like to get shocked*, I thought, *he wouldn't be so callous.* I never went back to that physician again.

After spending most of March either in the hospital or confined to my home, it was time to get back on track and start living my life again. I slowly began to do simple things, like going to the movies or attending baseball games with friends.

By the end of April, after continued improvement, Dr. Bump was ready for me to undergo a cardiac stress test, which involves exercising on a treadmill or stationary bike at increasing rates of difficulty, during which time the blood flow and heart rate are monitored closely.

The test went well and I was given clearance to begin a slow exercise program. Now I could ride my bike and start jogging again with friends. I was beginning to get my confidence back; my driving restriction was lifted, and by the beginning of May, I was able to participate in a sixteen-mile cycle event called Ride the Rock before taking a much-needed vacation to Miami to see the Chicago Cubs and Bulls play. Come June, two days before my thirty-seventh birthday, I returned to work in a part-time capacity.

As my health continued to show signs of improvement, my next big goal was to participate in the Warrior Dash, a popular 5K obstacle race through grass and mud that tests your cardiovascular and muscular endurance. It was a wonderful weekend and I was enjoying life again.

The following Wednesday, I had tickets for one of the Chicago Cubs vs. Chicago White Sox Crosstown Classic baseball games at New Comiskey Park.

As I often do during baseball games, I snuck down to find better seats and wound up in the fourth row near the Cubs' dugout on the first base line. The Cubs' first baseman, Carlos Peña, hit a home run in the top of the sixth inning, making it a close game, with the White Sox leading by only one run. Then, in the bottom of the seventh inning, the White Sox hit a groundout, with the throw going to Peña at first base for the final out of the inning. As the Cubs' slugger was jogging to the dugout, he took the baseball out of his mitt and tossed it into the crowd—straight to me.

In all my years of attending baseball games with family and friends, it was the first time I'd caught a game ball as it entered the stands. Though the Cubs lost the game, I was on cloud nine; that was one of the best nights of my life. Things really were starting to look up.

▲▲ ▲▲ ▲▲

After a wonderful Fourth of July weekend, I had a follow-up appointment with Dr. Bump. For the first time since my heart dilemma began, I had no irregular heartbeats detected during my visit.

"You have no new occurrences," Dr. Bump said happily. "Everything looks good and I don't think you'll need to have another ablation."

It was music to my ears. Finally, I could chalk the spring's events up to a bad experience and move on.

Two days later, I had an appointment with Dr. Spear, who also confirmed that all was well.

The future was once again bright—so I thought.

Later that very same day, I was enjoying an outdoor dinner with a high school friend at a local restaurant when, all of a sudden, my heart began to race. Immediately, I knew something was wrong, and we were forced to end our dinner abruptly. As we were heading for the car, I began sweating profusely and couldn't continue walking, so my friend ran to get the car and came back to pick me up.

At this point, I was carrying a heart rate monitor with me everywhere I went. Once in the car, the measurements confirmed my feelings: my heart rate had elevated to more than 190 beats per minute. I was terrified, and had my friend begin driving to Christ Hospital.

While driving, I was able to page Dr. Spear, who promptly returned my call and encouraged me to stop at a pharmacy to pick up a medication to help slow my heart rate rather than go to the emergency room.

As I anxiously watched every beat on my heart rate monitor, my friend took me to the Walgreens just two blocks away from Christ Hospital. Entering the store, my terribly slow pace would have made the tortoise look like the hare.

As Dr. Spear instructed, I called him after arriving at the pharmacy around 9:50 p.m., ten minutes before it was closing, and put him on speakerphone with the pharmacist so they could speak directly.

As they were talking, my heart rate elevated up to 212 beats per minute. I knew from all my device checks that my defibrillator was set to go off whenever my heart rate exceeded 210 beats per minute.

"My defibrillator is gonna go off!" I said frantically as I left my phone on the counter and scurried to a chair a few feet away.

WHAM!!! My defibrillator fired, sending a jolt of electricity to my heart, a quick flinch throughout my body, and a brief burst of sound from my mouth.

Immediately, the pharmacist got off the phone with Dr. Spear and called 911. The paramedics were there within five minutes, but the physical terror was over. Unlike back in March, the leads and device worked properly this time, so I only received one shock—not eighteen. My heart went back to a normal sinus rhythm, the perspiration stopped, and the physical aspect of the emergency was over. The emotional effects, however, were back in full force as the paramedics helped me into the stretcher and took me to the hospital only blocks away.

I was in the hospital for four days as my physicians altered my medications once again and tried to determine next steps. Both Dr. Bump and Dr. Spear visited, each expressing their concern and empathy regarding what had happened.

By the time I was released from the hospital, it was clear I would need a second ablation. This time, I left the hospital with a gift of sorts: Dr. Bump had given me a doughnut-shaped magnet that I could place over my defibrillator to disable it from firing. Having the ability to control the unnecessary shocks was a huge relief.

My next TEE procedure and ablation were scheduled for the following Monday.

⛰ ⛰ ⛰

That Saturday night, after confining myself to my home all week, I was getting ready to join my Meetup friends at an outdoor bar to celebrate the group leader's birthday. As I pulled into the parking lot, I could see everyone outside at the bar since the entire area was lit up from the lights of the outdoor sand volleyball courts on the premises.

Just after I parked and began to walk toward the party, my heart started to race erratically. It felt like a machine gun was going off in my chest. I took the magnet from my pocket and placed it over my chest to keep my device from firing and called 911. Fearing I'd pass out and collapse on the concrete sidewalk, I took a few quick steps and jumped in between a pile of bushes outside the fence that enclosed the bar and volleyball courts. I remained buried in the bushes until the paramedics arrived.

When the paramedics showed up, everyone from the party saw the ambulance and fire truck and wondered what the commotion was. A few of them walked out to see what was going on and realized it was me. I was horrified. The first time I've left my house in a week and I end up embarrassing myself in front of fifty-plus people by diving into a set of bushes and calling 911.

Meanwhile, the paramedics were trying to get me to let go of the magnet and remove it from my chest, but I refused and pleaded with them. I'm quite certain they had never experienced a call like that before, but I knew what would happen if I removed the magnet.

By the time I arrived at Palos Community Hospital, I had informed the paramedics and physicians of my scheduled ablation for Monday at Advocate Christ Medical Center, so I was transported by ambulance from one hospital to the other. Somewhere in the middle of all that was happening, I lost my fear about the procedures and surgeries themselves. I was too frustrated with the process to be scared.

How long will I have to endure and suffer like this? I wondered. *When will everything be better and back to normal?*

Not anytime soon.

In the midst of the TEE on Monday morning, with a tube down my throat and surrounded by medical staff, my heart went into tachycardia and began racing while I was on the stretcher. Unfortunately, I was not completely sedated and came to in the midst of everything happening. The doctor had to call a crash cart since my device was disabled for the procedure, and I watched as medical staff members raced frantically in and out of the room. The physician was concerned about whether or not Dr. Spear would still be able to perform the ablation with my heart racing the way it was, even though once he was involved in the procedure, that's exactly what Dr. Spear would try to induce to identify and cauterize the parts of my heart that were beating inappropriately.

Dr. Spear was able to move forward with the procedure. This time it took more than six hours to perform. When he came to see me in recovery and said all went well, a feeling of déjà vu washed over me. I hoped he was right.

I was released from the hospital on Wednesday; on Friday morning, my heart went into atrial tachycardia again. Placing my magnet over my chest to prevent another shock, I called 911.

▲▲ ▲▲ ▲▲

Dr. Spear came to see me at the hospital right away.

"The ablation didn't work," he admitted. "I thought we had it."

Dr. Spear continued to explain how multiple ablations are not uncommon, and he and my other two cardiologists, Drs. McNally and Bump, felt another ablation should be attempted before reviewing other options.

After an ablation, the laser-cauterized tissue in the heart needs time to heal or scar over. It's similar to a cut on the body needing to scab in order to stop the bleeding. Though the heart is usually given months to heal after an ablation, my cardiologists agreed that another procedure could be done sooner rather than later.

In August, after conducting a great deal of research, including a visit to the number one heart hospital in the country, Cleveland Clinic in Ohio, I was encouraged to have my third ablation done by a renowned electrophysiologist at The University of Chicago Hospital.

Dr. Burke, a mild-mannered physician with a good sense of humor, and his team of physicians spent more than eight hours trying to remedy the irregular heart rhythms that had plagued me for almost half the year. When it was done, Dr. Burke commented on how well the ablation had gone and said he was optimistic about the results. I'd heard that before.

To cope with all I had been through and get some additional support after my third ablation, I focused my attention on building relationships with people who were going through some of the same ordeals I was. After participating in the ICD Sports Registry research study out of Yale University, which was examining the activity levels of patients with ICDs, I was introduced to Young Hearts with ICDs, a group out of University of Iowa Hospital.

After speaking with a sonographer and nurse specialist who were in charge of the group's annual conference in Iowa, I was asked to share my story in September 2011.

During an open question-and-answer session later in the day, I learned that my nineteen shocks were more than anyone else in the room had ever experienced—not necessarily the type of contest I'd like to win. Moreover, I was the only person in the room with a defibrillator implanted from each of the three leading ICD manufacturers. While my situation was unique, I believe every single person in the room had a different experience to share. I felt honored to be a part of this community, and felt a deep connection with those involved. Meeting other patients with ICDs who could comprehend my ordeal, along with their family and friends, was amazing.

Since that meeting, I have led the young men's group at the annual conference in Iowa every year and have participated in other ICD groups as well. One of the most important lessons we learn there is that we're not alone. The people I've met and the stories I've heard have been an inspiration in my recovery and healing.

A month after the conference, it happened again: I began having blackout spells one morning. These feelings, though, were completely different from what I had been experiencing since my first ablation. I didn't feel a rapid heart rate in my chest; instead, it was reminiscent of what I dealt with years earlier before the first defibrillator was implanted. All of a sudden, I would simply begin to black out for a second or two, then the feeling would go away. It was troubling.

I was on the phone explaining the issue to Carrie, an advanced practice nurse at Dr. Burke's office, when I had another attack.

"Dr. Burke wants to see the kind of episodes you're having—if they're longer episodes or shorter ones like you were having before," Carrie was saying.

As she was finishing her sentence, I belted out in pain and crashed to the ground. My defibrillator had just fired. This was the second time this had happened to me while I was on the phone with a medical professional.

I lay in the middle of my kitchen floor, breathing heavily and full of fear, but still holding my phone. "My defibrillator just went off," I told Carrie.

"Your defibrillator went off?" she confirmed, a note of alarm in her voice. "Then you need to go to the hospital. Are you alone? Do you need me to call 911?"

Thankfully, I was not alone and had a friend in town from Europe. I hung up with Carrie and called 911—my fifth time doing so in less than seven months.

▲▲ ▲▲ ▲▲

I was in Palos Hospital for three days before they released me; the following Monday, Dr. Burke and I began making arrangements for a different type of surgery: a mini-maze procedure, which combines a traditional ablation with a newer epicardial technique. We got Dr. Shahab Akhter, a thoracic and cardiac surgeon of University of Chicago, to help do the job.

In the mini-maze procedure, the electrophysiologist and cardiac surgeon—Dr. Burke and Dr. Akhter, in this case—work side by side, ablating both the internal and external walls of the atrium. This time they would once again cauterize inappropriate rhythms in my heart through my veins using the femoral artery near my groin, and also simultaneously access other portions of my heart through incisions between my ribs. (Using the band analogy from before, rather than simply eliminating the band member playing out of tune using a laser pointed from the audience, the surgeon would simultaneously go undercover in the band through incisions in my rib cage to obtain a different angle on the band member.)

All of us hoped this hybrid approach would eradicate the consistent rapid heartbeats I continued to suffer.

Though this kind of procedure carried a higher success rate than a simple ablation, it also included a greater risk. In addition to opening wounds in my groin, ribs, and neck, Dr. Akhter would have to collapse my lung to gain better access to my heart.

After more than seven hours of surgery with two leading cardiac doctors, I found myself on the front end of another painful recovery. I was instructed to remain immobile due to the groin punctures and was connected with drainage tubes and wires. I felt like a dump truck had double-parked on my chest. The pain was far greater than what I had endured after the previous ablations, but a part of me felt if I was in that much pain, my doctors must have done a good job eliminating the cause for the unnecessary rhythms.

I spent almost a week recovering in the hospital, but my physicians immediately confirmed the surgery had been a success. I had heard that many times before, however, so I was a bit skeptical.

I had brought a Bears shirt with me to the hospital, having every intent to watch the game on Sunday. As fate would have it, the Bears' starting quarterback, Jay Cutler, broke his thumb during the game, and I was informed by staff members later that evening that he had made a visit to the ICU I had just been transferred out of and stopped to greet many of the patients on the floor before leaving. It's the only situation I can think of where I wish my improvement could have been delayed a little longer; I was really disappointed by the missed opportunity to have met him.

I was released from the hospital after a week—on oxygen, to assist with breathing problems I was having from the surgery—only to return two days later with fluid buildup and high carbon dioxide discharge from my lungs. I had developed an infection and a bad case of pneumonia due to pulmonary issues that are not uncommon with mini-maze procedures. In two weeks, I spent twelve out of fourteen days at University of Chicago Hospital.

On December 1, however, I was back home from the hospital, and this time I remained there. Finally, I was on the mend.

▲▲ ▲▲ ▲▲

As the New Year approached, I tried to leave my troubles from 2011— including the twenty ICD shocks, five cardiac surgeries, seven ER visits, seven hospital stays, six ambulance rides, five calls to 911, and collapsed lung—behind. After everything that happened, 2011 had taught me an invaluable lesson: more than any other year, it had taught me how life could change at any moment. I was either going to die or I was going to live, and I was determined to live before I died.

I harnessed my energy to move forward in 2012 and beyond.

After having been out on long-term disability for almost a year, in February I returned to work in a full-time capacity. My team and organization welcomed me back with open arms.

Though I suffered post-traumatic stress from all the shocks I'd received from my ICD and carried a magnet with me constantly, my cardiac rehabilitation had begun. I was back to exercising at the gym and pushing myself to new limits. Dr. McNally, thinking outside the box, even suggested I wear a Holter monitor for three days and participate in all types of activities—hiking, lifting, running, and any other personal activity, anything that would elevate my heart rate—to see what the effects were.

Over the course of the past year, I had grown accustomed to inching forward and getting knocked back. So, after three days of pushing my activity levels with a Holter monitor, I was excited to hear there were no abnormalities. After five months of continued progression, I attempted my first 5K in more than a year, the Race to Wrigley.

A 5K, which works out to be 3.1 miles, is more or less a beginner's race, but it does take time and training—and a strong heart. I'd run my first race the summer before Antarctica, but it was difficult. I found it really discouraging that my health issues had made my legs and heart so weak that running such a simple race was a challenge. At the same time, I loved having the challenge to live for.

The running itself wasn't such a problem, I'd discovered; it was the recuperation, which was slower than I was used to. Every effort I made to train, no matter how well I paced myself, brought on the painful reminder that my body was seriously damaged.

However, the alternative—not even trying—was unacceptable. I had to go beyond my comfort zone.

I was not able to finish the Race to Wrigley, which commences and ends near the famous Wrigley Field Marquee, without walking—it was now more than my body could handle—but that didn't keep me from trying. Before and after the race, I often thought about Peter Hillary's talk on the cruise to Antarctica. Here was a man who had seized life and made the most of it. Here was a man who knew that life is about facing challenges, not being defeated by them. It inspired me to keep pushing myself.

So, when the phone rang in the summer of 2012 and Chris was

on the other line asking if I'd be interested in joining her for a trek to Mount Everest, it immediately captured my interest.

"I can't climb Mount Everest," I joked, knowing that wasn't what she meant.

"Not climb," she explained. "It's a hike up to the base camp."

"What does that entail?"

"We start off in the mountains around 10,000 feet and hike up to Base Camp at 17,600 feet; it would be a huge accomplishment."

After about fifteen minutes of discussing the idea, I hung up the phone thrilled: I had an awesome new goal. If what makes you a man is getting up after life kicks you down, then what better way to get up again than to climb up to the tallest mountain in the world?

Next, I just had to see what my physicians thought of the idea.

CHAPTER 12:

MOUNTAIN TRAINING

Start by doing what's necessary; then do what's possible, and
suddenly you are doing the impossible.

—Francis of Assisi

"Are you crazy?" my cardiologist, Dr. McNally, asked me. "Rob, you aren't in any shape to climb the stairs, much less Mount Everest."

She wasn't the first physician to express concern. Dr. Burke also had considered the trip irresponsible. Still, I wasn't about to be discouraged.

It was November 2012, and my body had finally recovered from the many blows of 2011. That same month, my mother died, which set me back emotionally, but as far as my health was concerned, I was in pretty decent shape, considering my diagnoses.

I'd been working with Dr. McNally since 2006. Not only was she an excellent cardiologist, she was an expert in evaluating muscular dystrophy and cardiomyopathy. Like Dr. Ferraro and several other doctors I'd worked with, she was the kind of physician who sat down with her patients and took the time to listen. However, when it came to me climbing Mount Everest, she wasn't willing to compromise—at least, not yet.

"Do you have any idea how dangerous mountain climbing is, even for someone who's healthy?" she asked me. "One of my best students died on a climbing expedition, and I don't want to see you do the same."

"But I—"

"No, Rob. Look, I love that you want to challenge yourself, but no extreme sports. Exercise, run, continue to play sports, but no mountain climbing. And whatever you do, train for something here; don't go to a Third World country where you'll have no access to the kind of care you might need. Understand?"

"I know, Dr. McNally, but if I train and don't overdo it, I think I can make it." I had gone into the appointment with a can-do attitude, and I wasn't backing down. I was confident that I could persuade her.

She just looked at me, her face half smiling but dead serious. "I'm not going to give you my blessing or clearance!"

That was the end of that conversation—but I wasn't about to give up. I tried talking to one of my other doctors, then another, and another. Each time, I got the same response. Only one of my physicians was willing to support the trip; of the many who were not, one even suggested that if I went ahead and tried climbing Mount Everest, they might not continue to treat me. In the end, it was pretty obvious I should just leave it alone. However, that is not my nature.

Just a few years before, in 2010, I'd had a similar experience when trying to get clearance to scuba dive for the first time. There were uncertainties about what could take place underwater, and my doctors were reluctant to let me try. After much negotiation and research, it was determined that I could scuba dive as long as I went no deeper than one atmosphere—approximately thirty-three feet. In August of 2010, while on vacation, I went scuba diving for the first time in the district of Kona off the big island of Hawaii. It was an amazing experience, one I had to fight for, and it was so worth it.

I respect the knowledge and expertise of my physicians. At the same time, I realize that nobody knows my body and feelings better than I do—my ambitions, my drive, my pain, and my fight to overcome obstacles. Individually, neither the physicians who care for me nor I alone can make the best decision. Collectively, however, combining their wisdom and my zest for life, we can.

Finally, Dr. McNally said something that gave me hope: "Rob, if you can be healthy for an entire year, we can talk about this. I'm not making any promises, but if your condition improves and there are no more incidents, we can discuss it."

That was enough for me. That became my goal: to get back into suitable shape and have faith that nothing bad would happen to me in the coming year. So I began training. I began eating better than I ever had in my life and started exercising with a passion—but a tempered passion. I knew I had to pace myself and not overdo it. I had a goal, and that was all I needed to motivate me into action.

In the meantime, Chris went to Nepal and hiked to Everest Base Camp without me.

"It was amazing," she said when she returned.

"What was it like?" I was super excited to hear about it, though it hurt. I really wished I could have gone with her.

"Oh, Robby, it was a bitch. It was the most difficult thing I've ever done."

▲▲ ▲▲ ▲▲

Once I heard about the trip and how difficult it was, I was even more determined to do it myself, as soon as I was able. Fueled by my own adrenaline, I spent the next twelve months stretching, running, and lifting weights. I monitored my heart religiously, took my meds as prescribed, and ate a high-protein, low-fat diet while doing my best to keep a positive attitude when all else seemed hopeless. When I wasn't working or working out, I was talking to people or watching films about Mount Everest.

The more I learned, the more in awe I was of all the men and women who had scaled that mountain—each one had worked hard and persevered and reached their goal. Even those who hadn't reached the top had equally amazing stories to tell. Those who had survived, at least. About 250 people have died trying to reach Everest's summit, from hypothermia, altitude sickness, falls through crevices so deep they may never have landed, and natural disasters, including blizzards, avalanches, and earthquakes. Many of them have died just trying to reach Everest Base Camp. It wasn't going to be an easy adventure, that was for sure.

In the meantime, I was in the midst of a relationship with a wonderful woman named Kathy. We had met on Match.com, which is where I had met Diana and about 95 percent of the dates I'd been on since 2001.

Dating is hard enough for anybody, even more so when you have all the health issues I do. It was difficult to find someone who would be a true partner, and the women I met usually fell into two categories: the Caretakers, who want to do everything to help take care of you, and the Runaways, who think you're damaged goods so they go AWOL the second they find out about your medical condition.

Kathy, who fell in the Caretaker category, was a shy woman with an extremely strong undertone. She had raised her six-year-old son and puppy essentially by herself, and they were great. She was natural and beautiful—she had radiant eyes, an amazing figure, and incredible demeanor. We really hit it off, and she gave me the inspiration I needed to keep going.

And the truth is, I really needed that kind of inspiration. Just making it through the day without an incident while also juggling my training, a full-time job, and a relationship felt like a mountain to conquer. But I felt up to the challenge.

▲▲ ▲▲ ▲▲

The year of 2014 was important to me on many levels. It was a year of overcoming obstacles and living my life to the fullest.

First, I would be celebrating my fortieth birthday on June 8th. Kathy and her son, whom I'd grown close to, helped me arrange a birthday celebration with several friends and family at a local bowling alley with a large outdoor space that included a couple of sand volleyball courts. We had great food, played volleyball and games for hours, and the sun smiled down on us the entire time. It was a beautiful day.

My birthday weekend also included a Cubs game, where I got the opportunity to meet a legend: Lennie Merullo, the last living member of the Chicago Cubs to play in the 1945 World Series. He was a great guy, and we spoke briefly about my health issues and our lifelong love of the Cubs.

Days later, I went back to Wrigley Field for Family Day, an annual event where the Cubs allow season ticket holders to go onto the field. It was a perfect sunny day with the short grass under my feet, as I reminisced about attending games with my dad and grandpa back when I was a kid.

Finally, the month of June ended with me and Kathy taking an eight-day Caribbean cruise out of New York. It was the first time I'd been back to New York since the Freedom Tower was completed. In 2001, I had taken a nice picture from the Statue of Liberty with the World Trade Center in the background, not knowing it was the last time I would see it. After the attack on 9/11, I went back and saw the remains of the disaster. When Kathy and I cruised past the Freedom Tower, what really impacted me was what it represented: something that had gotten knocked down in such a tragic and violent way but had been raised back up bigger and better than before. It really struck a chord with me and epitomized what I was trying to do.

The summer of conquering goals continued when I returned from the cruise in early July and flew to Washington, DC for the Fourth of July. For years I had wanted to celebrate Independence Day from our nation's capital and watch the fireworks from the Lincoln Memorial Reflective Pool in National Mall.

I showed up several hours early to walk around and make sure I had a good seat for the evening display. It was only the middle of the afternoon, but there were people everywhere—to my right on the steps of the Lincoln Memorial and to my left as far as my eyes could see, covering the grass near the Washington Memorial and Capitol building.

After hours of anticipation, the fireworks began, an elegant and impressive display. I could feel each explosion of the fireworks in the air as if it were my heart beating to a perfect rhythm in my chest. It was every bit as wonderful as I could have imagined.

▲▲ ▲▲ ▲▲

The summer was going so well, and since I hadn't had any problems for more than a year, I thought when I reintroduced the concept of climbing Mount Everest to my doctors, they'd all change their minds. Once they saw how healthy I'd become, I told myself, they'd be all for the idea. I was wrong.

"Running here is one thing, Rob," Dr. McNally told me, "but we don't know how your body will respond to higher altitudes. The higher you go, the less oxygen there is, and with muscular dystrophy, your muscles crave *more* oxygen." She shook her head. "You'd be in a Third World country; anything could happen, and you'd have no access to the type of care you'd need."

"Just because you've made it through one year without any problems doesn't mean you'll make it through a second year," another doctor cautioned. "You could still have heart problems at any moment, and there's no telling how quickly you might lose motor control from the muscular dystrophy."

They were right. I had no idea how my body would respond at high altitude, but I felt compelled to find out.

Then I learned about Steve Gleason, who played football for the New Orleans Saints and blocked the Atlanta Falcons' punt, leading to a touchdown for the Saints—the first points scored at the New Orleans Superdome in 2006. It was the first time the Saints had scored in the first quarter of a first home game in nearly two years, and that play became a symbol of recovery for post-Katrina New Orleans.

What really intrigued me about Steve Gleason was his announcement of being diagnosed in 2011 with amyotrophic lateral sclerosis (ALS)—aka Lou Gehrig's disease. ALS is a horrible disease: it progressively kills the motor neurons until eating, breathing, and even moving the eyes becomes impossible. ALS patients usually end up suffocating because they can't even control their own breathing.

Yet this devastating disease didn't stop Gleason, who planned a hiking expedition to Machu Picchu in 2013 to raise money for ALS research. To prepare, he underwent testing at a hyperbaric chamber at Duke University, where controlled pressure mimicked high altitude.

Hyperbaric chambers only test for minutes or hours, so they aren't an accurate indication of how the body will survive over days and weeks at high altitude. However, Gleason was an adventurer, and he was determined, so he put together a team—and ultimately, with their help, he made it up the mountain. Team Gleason went even further after that, planning white water rafting trips in Italy, cruising the Panama Canal, and attending Super Bowl games—all for people with

ALS. Nothing stopped Gleason from living a full life. If he could do it, so would I.

I called the Center for Hyperbaric Medicine and Environmental Physiology at Duke University. When I told them about my medical history and my plans to climb Mount Everest, the physicians I spoke with were very excited. When I shared the information with Dr. McNally, though, she was less than enthused.

"Rob," she said, "hyperbaric chambers aren't the same as climbing mountains. They can't replicate sleeping and waking at high altitudes or going hiking day after day."

"Then what do you suggest I do?" I asked her. "I'm going to do this trip, so what do I need to do to be prepared? If it isn't a hyperbaric chamber, what do you suggest?"

"I suggest you find something more in line with what your body will go through if you climb to the base camp of Mount Everest. I recommend you forget the whole thing, but if you're not going to do that, then start climbing some mountains here."

"Where?" I asked.

"Maybe Colorado. Find some high-altitude destinations in the US and start from there. At least you'll have access to appropriate healthcare if something goes wrong."

"All right, doc," I said. "That's what I'll do!"

After leaving her office, there was only one thing to do: climb some mountains.

⛰ ⛰ ⛰

I went online and looked up the city with the highest altitude in the continental US. It turned out to be Alma, Colorado, an old mining town with an elevation of 10,578 feet and a subarctic climate. With a population of less than two hundred, I figured it was pretty much a ghost town. Like Sylvester Stallone going to Russia in *Rocky IV*, it was the perfect place to train. If I couldn't make it in Alma, Colorado, there was no way I'd be able to do something like hike the 18,000 feet to Everest Base Camp.

I wasn't a complete novice when it came to high altitude. I had taken a sunrise bike tour on Mount Haleakala in Hawaii back in 2010 and hiked around Mauna Kea, which is almost 14,000 feet. However, I hadn't done any high-altitude hiking since my health problems began in 2011. So in order to prepare for the hike up Alma—a trek that would be a test of my tweaked, less vigorous heart—Kathy and I took a trip to Washington State and Vancouver, Canada, to do some elevation training and vacationing. While in Vancouver, we saw the largest offshore fireworks competition in the world, and, in order to complete my goal, watched a home game in my thirtieth and final Major League Baseball stadium at Safeco Field in Seattle, which culminated with MLB conducting an interview of me during the game.

The first hike of the trip was on Grouse Mountain in Vancouver. I was really excited to visit the area, as it is well known for being the site of the 2010 Winter Olympics. The particular trail we hiked, The Grouse Grind, may only be about two miles in length, but with an elevation gain of almost 3,000 feet, it has been called "Mother Nature's Stairmaster"— and it was definitely a grind.

Kathy and I struggled to complete The Grouse Grind, and took many breaks while heading up the trail. It was clear that much more work would need to be done to prepare for something as big as Mount Everest. By the end of the climb, I was exhausted and yet relieved at the same time. After finishing the trail, we took a ski lift and walked farther up the mountain for some sightseeing at the Eye of the Wind, the world's first wind-powered turbine allowing visitors to stand in a 360-degree glass pod to view the area, almost three hundred feet above the turbine's base.

After Canada, the next stop was Mount St. Helens, which has an elevation of more than 5,000 feet. As a kid, I remember learning of the eruption in 1980. I'd always wanted to visit. Now I was getting my chance.

The eight-mile hike to Harry's Ridge was much different from Grouse Grind—the sun and heat were the largest obstacles. One part of the trail, called "The Devil's Elbow," was very narrow and had a tight curve along the side of the mountain with a steep drop-off. It was scary and dangerous, but amazing.

"I can't make it," Kathy exclaimed during one part of the hike. The heat was getting to her, and she was discouraged. She waved a hand. "Go on without me."

"You can do it," I said. "If I can do it, you can do it." I took her by the hand. "We don't have that much further to go."

She begrudgingly continued, and together we persisted—fighting the elements and battling through the rugged terrain—until we reached Harry's Ridge, where we squeezed each other with hugs.

"Thank you for pushing me," Kathy said.

"Thank you!" I returned with love. "I wouldn't be here without you!"

The last hike of the trip was on Burroughs Mountain, often described as a mountain against a mountain, as it has dramatic, uninhibited views of Mount Rainier. It would increase our hiking altitude to almost 8,000 feet.

This hike was different from the others, with the pristine view of Mount Rainier always in sight. Similar to a dream, it seemed no matter how long we hiked, we didn't appear to move or get any closer. Even with snow on parts of the trail along the way, it wasn't very cold, and we had a steady incline before turning around Second Burroughs.

Each of these hikes provided a very different experience and offered a diverse perspective regarding the types of challenges I would plan to encounter on my expedition to Mount Everest.

One obstacle remained in my path: I needed to spend five or more days at 10,000-plus feet—eating, hiking, and sleeping. If I could do that, my doctors would support me trying something more. I was so excited; it was time to head to Alma!

CHAPTER 13:

ALTITUDE AND ATTITUDE

Very often what God first helps us towards is not the virtue
itself, but just this power of always trying again.

—C. S. Lewis

The original plan was for a friend to join me for my hiking trip to Alma. At the last minute, however, she canceled and left me with two choices: go it alone or don't go at all. I decided I'd go alone and moved the trip from October to November—a decision that proved to have crucial consequences.

The drive up to Alma was dazzling, with nothing but mountain peaks, pine trees, brilliant blue skies, and icy grey rivers wherever you look. Eagles flew overhead like omens of good fortune, blessing my journey, and I couldn't have been more excited as I drove higher and higher toward my goal.

Alma is an old silver mining town that was fairly prosperous in the nineteenth century. They used to produce over one and a half million pounds of silver each year, but a smallpox epidemic in 1861 pretty much wiped out the town. Now all that's left of Alma is a handful of families, many of whom mine rhodochrosite, a bright red mineral used as an alloy in stainless steel and aluminum. Many also provide services to tourists like me, who want to hike any of the three 14,000-foot peaks in the area (aka the fourteeners) or visit one of the two local ski resorts.

I had tried to exercise due diligence in lining up a place to stay before I arrived in Alma. What I learned was that there was only one hotel in town, aptly named the No Name Hotel. When I called to make my reservation, the person I spoke with assured me the rooms had a bathroom, heat, and Wi-Fi, along with whatever else I'd need.

What I hadn't anticipated was just how out of place I'd be once I got to Alma. Most of the people living in this small, rugged, frigid environment seemed like back-to-nature kind of people—long-haired pot smokers who lived off the grid. We couldn't have been more different, so it wasn't long before I felt pretty uncomfortable and conspicuously out of place.

When I arrived at the hotel, I went into the bar area, where the bartender/hotel manager was.

"What do you need?" he asked abruptly.

"Hi, my name is Rob Besecker," I said with a smile. "I've got a reservation."

He was sort of rough around the edges, but a laid-back type with a long ponytail. For some reason, I just didn't feel comfortable with him. I guess I didn't do a good job of concealing my nervousness, because he didn't exactly seem overjoyed to see me either.

"What brings you here?" he asked, seeming skeptical.

"I'm training for a hike to Mount Everest, and I came out here to acclimate to the high altitude."

His attitude shifted, and he suddenly looked impressed and intrigued. He was surprised to see a tourist at that time of year. Ski season hadn't yet begun, and he'd had no idea why I'd want to be there if not to ski.

"We got you upstairs," he said, handing me the room key and giving back my credit card.

I stayed in the bar to catch the end of the afternoon football game, ordering a pop and chatting a bit with some others also watching the game.

Maybe this won't be so bad after all, I thought as I grabbed my gear from the car and hauled it to my room.

▲▲　▲▲　▲▲

A ray of light from the setting sun was falling across the bed when I opened the door to my room, illuminating blankets of dust that hung in the air like dying stars. There was a dresser, of sorts, and a bedside table. Not much else.

The room was the size of a king-size bed, and it was freezing. I threw my bags on the bed and turned around, looking for the bathroom. When I found a door, I opened it, only to see a tiny closet not much bigger than an ironing board.

All of a sudden, it became clear to me: I'd asked if the rooms had heat, but I hadn't asked whether it would be turned on. I'd asked if each room had a bathroom and shower, but I hadn't asked whether it was shared with the rest of the hotel. I'd asked if they had working Wi-Fi in the rooms, but I hadn't asked if it worked regularly.

I was extremely disappointed. I felt so uncomfortable, so out of place. The raucous cheers and shouts from the bar down below were getting louder with the drinking, smoking, and partying, and I was just this clean-cut kid from the Midwest who only wanted to take a hot shower and rest before the Sunday night football game. The more I thought about it, the more out of place and uncomfortable I felt in this hole-in-the wall room with no heat, no shower, not even a toilet. I wanted to leave.

An unexplainable fear manifested itself in me that checking out would be an issue. To prepare for the worst, I went to the end of the hallway and crawled down the fire escape so no one would see me putting my bags back in the car; then I could make a quick getaway if there were any problems. I felt like a child sneaking out of the house to avoid detection; it was ridiculous, but it was all I could do to calm my nerves. Then I returned to the bar to speak with the manager.

"Excuse me," I said, grabbing his attention. "Do you mind if I check out?"

"Why?" he asked. "You've already paid for the room."

"Well, I'd like to get my money back and leave," I explained.

"No refunds," he said, confirming my fear that there may be a problem.

"What do you mean? I just gave you my credit card less than twenty minutes ago," I appealed. "I specifically called ahead of time and asked if each room had a bathroom, heat, and working Wi-Fi, and you don't. I'm just not comfortable staying here."

"There is a shared bathroom and shower down the hall," he said. "We've got Wi-Fi over there," he said, pointing to a corner in the bar. "It doesn't always work, but some days it does."

"Well, that's not what I came here for," I said, remaining calm but feeling like I was being taken for a ride. "I'd like a refund so I can leave and find something else."

He took a deep breath, shook his head, and turned his back to me, busying himself with other tasks. A moment later, he turned back to me and said, in a voice full of condescension, "You know, you're never going to make it to Everest if you can't handle staying here."

"I just want my money back," I calmly repeated.

Finally, he gave in, but since it was not a computerized system, canceling the credit card transaction seemed to take forever. After fifteen frustrating minutes, with everyone in the small hotel bar staring at me, I got my money back and left.

Once in my car, however, I had to find somewhere else to stay. Like the Hotel California, I had just checked out, but it seemed I could never leave. There was no other hotel in Alma.

As I turned the key and started the engine, I remembered Fairplay, the small town I had passed through about five miles down the road, and headed there.

It was getting dark when I pulled into Fairplay, a town straight out of an old Western movie. I didn't have to go far before I saw a big sign that said "HOTEL," so I parked the car and went inside.

It looked like the Bates Motel on steroids—quite large, which was a surprise in such a small town. It had to be better than the last place. I walked up to the front desk and explained my dilemma to the guy behind the front desk, who was really nice and understanding.

"It's a different breed of people up there," he explained.

I felt much more at ease, as if I'd already had that soothing shower I so badly wanted.

▲▲ ▲▲ ▲▲

That night, I walked through what seemed like a ghost town to a bar down the street for the Sunday night football game and relaxed a little. When I got back to the hotel and my room later that evening, the heat was out and it was freezing cold—and the Wi-Fi wasn't working.

I was tired of being disappointed, tired of arguing over amenities, and still upset by the guy in Alma. I just wanted to sleep, so I went to bed in my snow gear and buried myself in the blankets.

Why is the guy from Alma still bugging me? I wondered. *What does he know about hiking Mount Everest? What does he know about anything?*

I realized what was really bothering me was that there was some truth behind what he'd said. If I couldn't handle a bathroom down the hall in Alma, Colorado, how was I going to handle an outhouse in the Himalayas?

On the other hand, I wasn't in Nepal yet, and I was paying for these minor conveniences.

Damn straight I want a room with heat and a bathroom, I thought as I drifted off to sleep.

▲▲ ▲▲ ▲▲

The next morning, I went downstairs to work on my computer in the foyer and told the front desk the heat in my room was out. Then I focused on getting my mind settled: I started to accept that I was in for some rough living over the next couple of days. I thought back to that sermon about detours, about how sometimes things just don't go the way we've planned. My trip to Colorado was certainly falling into that category, but as long as I could keep my focus on the positive and accept that I couldn't control everything about the trip, I knew I'd be all right.

That's easier said than done, however. Try as I might to calm down, the buildup of frustration and disappointment was beginning to take a toll on me. As I sat there checking email and ruminating on the detours

I'd run into, I realized that I'd long been harboring a tremendous anger—an anger that I had to live with such a damaged body. I hadn't really thought about my anger before, but now I recognized that it was there, right beneath the surface.

How much of that anger had driven Diana away? My sisters away? Even friends away? Was I the only one unaware of how angry I'd been ever since my diagnoses? Hell, for that matter, I'd been angry for as long as I could remember, but especially after breaking my back and not getting to play college football. All those years I'd smiled at the doctors, shrugged off the limitations of my life as if they were no big deal, and cared for my seriously ill parents, I'd been lying to myself. I'd been pretending it was no big deal when it was all a very big deal—and I was pissed off that it had happened to me. I was pissed off that it had happened to my family, and I was pissed off that it happened to anyone at all. I was beginning to realize: I was pissed off.

Then, just as suddenly as those thoughts had entered my mind, I also realized all those disappointments in my life were nobody's fault.

I don't blame my parents for my bad genes, I don't blame God for this happening to me, and I don't blame myself for not having a better body. It's not my fault. It's nobody's fault. These are just detours, and here I am in Colorado, having another detour.

With those thoughts in my head, I smiled and got ready for my day. I had some training to do.

▲▲ ▲▲ ▲▲

My first stop was a sports shop down the street. Some guys from the bar had recommended speaking with the owner about good hiking in the area. The meeting didn't end up as promising as I'd hoped, unfortunately. He gave me a map but told me it was a horrible time to hike. Due to all the snow the previous week, all the nearby trails were closed.

"You can't go hiking in this weather," he said. "All this snow, you could get stuck out there, might never be found. It's too dangerous!"

I could drive thirty minutes down the mountain to hike, he said— but I wasn't there for hiking, I was there for the elevation. Going down the mountain to hike wasn't an option.

This is just great, I thought. *Everything's a bust! Not one damned thing's gone right since I got here.*

No sooner had those thoughts gone through my mind than I shooed them away. *I'm in Colorado, and it's beautiful. I'm here to exercise and sleep at high elevation. I'm already at high elevation. I just need to exercise. I don't need to hike to a 14,000-foot peak to prove to my doctors that I can hike in Nepal. I just have to prove my body and heart can withstand the high altitude. Yeah, the trip hasn't been the greatest, but isn't that why I came—to overcome adversity? I didn't come here to have a good time; I came here to condition my body and mind. That's exactly what I'm doing, making the best of a bad situation.*

I started with a five-mile hike that afternoon at a little creek a couple of miles away called Beaver Creek. Although the route itself was not overly impressive, the backdrop of mountains in the background, along with the sunshine barreling through the frigid cold, made for a peaceful day. It was another reminder that it's not all about the destination, and I needed to enjoy the journey.

It was a nice uphill hike on the way there, and it felt great. The air was crisp and clean, and I couldn't have felt better. I wasn't angry at anyone, not even disappointed. Instead, I was very much aware of how blessed I was to be doing exactly what I set out to do—hike and eat and sleep for days in one of the highest places in the country. What was so bad about that?

Later in the day, I drove to a local brewery in town and struck up a conversation with the only other patron there, who happened to be the owner of the local bowling alley. Like everyone in town, he was curious what had brought me to the area. He was a very nice guy, and ended up inviting me to stop by his bowling alley later that evening for dinner and Monday Night Football. He also insisted on buying me a drink.

Though I had completely eliminated consuming caffeine and alcohol after being diagnosed with my heart conditions in 2000, after having a drink to celebrate the twenty-first birthday of my goddaughter—my oldest niece—in 2012, and seeing that it did not have an adverse effect on my heart, I'd realized I could occasionally allow myself to indulge in an adult beverage or two. So I accepted the beer, raised my glass in salute to my friendly acquaintance, and had a pleasant time with him. Clearly, once I'd changed my attitude about the day, the day had gotten better.

Later that evening, I went to the bowling alley down the street. In no time, the owner and I were chatting it up again. I was having a great time—eating tamales in a tiny little bowling alley, hanging out with some friendly people in this nice family town, watching the football game— when I noticed some unfriendly faces. They belonged to some of the guys I'd met in Alma. They were bowling, and every now and then they'd look at me. I'd look right back at them. Nobody said anything, but I felt like I was back in the Wild West. These were the guys in black hats, and I was keeping my eye on them, just as they were keeping their eyes on me. I didn't mind. In fact, it made the evening all the more enjoyable. Nothing could have been more fun at that point in the trip, and everything had seemed to turn around as if by magic—I was having a blast.

The next morning, I went to the park ranger station and asked for more suggestions on places to hike in the area.

"Well . . ." the ranger said, drawing out the word like it was a sentence all its own. "You don't want to go to the fourteeners," he said, referring to the trails with an elevation of 14,000 feet. "Those hiking trails are closed right now; too much snow."

"So where can I go?" I asked, eager to get my legs moving.

"If you drive south a bit to where it's not so high, you'll find lots of trails where you can get in a good hike." He showed me some spots on the map where he said the trails were clear.

"What about here?" I said, pointing to a spot not too far from where we were. It was a reservoir, and I wondered if that might be a good scenic place to go.

"Oh, that's the Fairplay Beach Reservoir and Recreational Area. It's got some pretty steep steps that go down to the reservoir, and climbing up and down those will give you a good workout. Even so, I wouldn't go there if I were you; it's not very interesting. You should drive a little farther out; you'll find some nice places if you go lower in altitude."

Nobody seemed to understand that I didn't care as much about the scenery and needed to remain at the higher altitude, so I finally just nodded and moved forward with my own agenda.

Hiking at the reservoir was beautiful. The sky was crystal clear, the snow iridescent, and the mountains in the distance spectacular. The reservoir itself was frozen over, but there was a nice trail surrounding it. I immediately noticed the stairs the ranger had told me about, and figured this would be a perfect way to work out.

I started by doing a mile lap around the reservoir on the trail. Next, I began pacing back and forth over a couple-hundred-yard stretch that included a steep hill on one side, the steep stairs on the other, and a wooden bridge right in the middle. It was repetitive but nice, and I immediately began to work up a sweat. Next, I focused on the stairs and did another twenty laps up and down them, with push-ups and pull-ups on the handrails after each lap. By the time I was done, I was fatigued and energized at the same time.

When I finished, it was still early in the day, so I decided to go for a drive in the mountains. As I drove through the winding roads with hawks and eagles flying overhead, I found myself thoroughly enchanted.

It wasn't long before the roads became narrower and the snow got deeper, and there were fewer and fewer cars. I realized I was driving into oblivion. If a snowstorm hit or something happened, I could get stuck. *I'd better turn around*, I thought.

I turned the steering wheel left to make a U-turn. Unfortunately, the snow was already deeper than I'd anticipated, and before I knew what was happening, my car was stuck in the middle of the road, the U-turn incomplete.

At first, I thought nothing of it. It was a minor inconvenience on an otherwise gorgeous day. I started rocking the car back and forth by moving just inches forward, then inches back. That only dug me in deeper, however, and in no time my wheels were spinning.

How was I going to get out of there? It was about one or two in the afternoon and the sun would be setting in a couple of hours; by four thirty or so it would be pitch-black.

I pulled out my cell phone to call for help, only to discover there was no service.

"Damn!" I said out loud. "Why did I do this?" I laughed at myself for driving into the mountains, where cell phone service was patchy at best. I was such a rookie in the mountains.

All this time, I'd been thinking that I had to get my body into shape, but I'd never really considered that even in the best of shape, people die on mountains. I realized in that moment how often humans underestimate the powerful force of the earth—and overestimate cell phone signals.

It wasn't my body I needed to be working better at that moment, it was my damn cell phone! I got a weak signal and tried calling the hotel, but the signal died out before I could get through.

Am I going to get stuck and freeze to death up here? I began to worry. Surely not. Surely, I'd be able to keep warm enough through the night and hang on until someone came along.

But what if I couldn't? What if my heart couldn't take a night in such a high altitude without any heat? If I'd come in October, as I'd originally planned, this never would have happened. There wouldn't have been this much snow.

These thoughts filtered through my mind, but every time, I batted them away. I can't say that I was terribly worried, but I was thinking that I ought to be. Here I was, out in the middle of nowhere, totally alone. I had probably driven eight or nine miles, so if worse came to worst, I could probably walk back. I had time to get to town before it got too late.

"I'll be okay," I muttered out loud. "I'll be okay."

I continued to fiddle with my cell phone and eventually got a signal and reached the hotel. The person I spoke with wanted to know where I was. My GPS wasn't working, so all I could do was walk to the closest street sign and do my best to describe the route I had taken to get there. They didn't seem happy, but said they'd send a tow truck.

I spent the next hour trying to dig myself out—even taking the floor mats out of my car and putting them under the tires for traction, and going into the nearby woods for branches to use as leverage to hoist the car over the hole the tires had dug into the snow. I kept thinking about that fine line between life and death, realizing how dependent I was on having a cell phone, on the hotel, even on luck.

Thankfully, I did have warm clothes, and shelter, too, even if my shelter was only my car. As the sun set lower and no tow truck had arrived, I began to think I might have to stay in my car after all; it was already too late to start walking.

Finally, after hours of waiting and wondering, a tow truck arrived. A big, lumbering guy got out of the truck and began to walk my way.

"You sure did get yerself in a mess out here, buddy," he said.

I was just so grateful to see him. I was pretty embarrassed and tried laughing it off. He wasn't laughing, though—he immediately recognized the potential danger of the situation and began to hook chains to my rental car.

It took him about five minutes to hook me up and pull me about ten feet forward out of the snow, and then I was able to drive away, having avoided that fine line separating life from death.

My trip to Alma reaffirmed an important message—that life can be taken away at any moment, with or without warning. My years in hospice care had emphasized the same point: Life is precious, so you shouldn't take any moment for granted. Enjoy every second.

CHAPTER 14:

THE LAST STRETCH

Strength does not come from physical capacity. It comes from an indomitable will.

—Mahatma Gandhi

When I returned to Chicago after my trip to Alma, I had a visit with Dr. Bump. He liked my Mount Everest idea but was also very cautious and had relied on the opinions of Drs. McNally and Burke since all my issues in 2011. He checked my pacemaker and defibrillator to see if Alma's high altitude had caused any issues and was pleased to see there were none.

"You look great, Rob," he said. "Congratulations! Keep up the good work!"

I left his office filled with optimism. Having his approval meant the world to me; it meant that someone who knew the weaknesses of my heart had faith that I could reach my goal of climbing to the base camp of Mount Everest. Next up was Dr. McNally. What would she think? She'd never liked the idea in the first place.

"Rob," she said, "I know you want to live your life to the fullest, and I'm happy to see you're doing that. I just don't want you to do anything silly. I'm glad to hear how well you did in Colorado. Keep me posted and don't run off to Mount Everest without checking in with us."

I left her office knowing she was more worried than enthusiastic, but her permission was enough for me. If she ever came right out and told me I couldn't go, I probably wouldn't, but as long as she gave me a cautious stamp of approval, my hike up Mount Everest was going to happen.

Dr. McNally was right about me needing to test myself at a high altitude before going. If there was one thing I'd gotten out of my trip to Colorado, it was the knowledge that my body could tolerate increased elevations. Throughout my time there, I'd been conscious of my heart and how my body was responding, yet I'd never felt overly short of breath or experienced any headaches. The trip had given me a lot more knowledge of myself and a lot more drive; it was the spark that had really gotten me going.

The experience also had given me a lot of confidence that I would be able to adjust to both the altitude and my own attitude. It had been, if anything, a wake-up call. My body was in good shape, but my attitude could use some help. If I could adjust that—and I knew I could—and get into even better shape, I could conquer Mount Everest.

▲ ▲ ▲

Gung-ho to get into the best possible physical and mental shape I could attain, I started by hitting my total body resistance (TRX) workouts really hard on Mondays, Wednesdays, and Fridays. TRX is a form of training in which you use suspension ropes anchored up above you for different movements, pulling against gravity and your body weight. I also went to the gym about three to five hours a week and hired a personal trainer. On weekends, I focused on cardiovascular training and hiking.

By breaking up my training into different types—the TRX, the gym, cardio work, and push-ups and sit-ups whenever I could squeeze them in—I was growing stronger every day. There were many days my body ached from the moment I woke up to the moment I went to sleep. I was sore and tired and didn't want to move. The snaps, crackles, and pops my body made when I got out of bed in the morning were enough to make the Rice Krispies characters jealous.

In order to persevere, I realized I had to pace myself, work within my limits, and listen to my body. I knew I couldn't train as I once had. I found that my body didn't do well with back-to-back workouts every day, so I started working out one day and resting or exercising lightly the next day. In the past, I would have likely been disappointed in myself for not tackling a workout every day, but my new body couldn't take that. By accepting my limits, I was steadily moving toward increasing them. By putting in at least five hours a week, I was growing stronger, and my measured approach was making it possible to get into amazing shape for the trip.

As for my mental state, I knew I needed to pace myself there as well, especially without an extensive support network to lean on. My dad had been gone for over five years by this point, and my mom for two. Chris and I were getting along again, but I was spending most of my time preparing for the trip and working out. Kathy was no longer in my life. Our relationship had fallen apart shortly after we returned from our trip to Washington State. Kathy had felt I was too involved in other areas of my life, and that I wasn't focused enough on her and her son. I was very surprised by the breakup and deeply saddened over losing her.

To keep the depression at bay, I became even more involved with additional philanthropic and advocacy organizations. I spent a lot of time reaching out to other people facing similar health issues, as well as advocates and experts, and attended many fundraisers and events in the fields of myotonic dystrophy and heart disease.

One of the groups that inspired me the most was the Stanford Neuromuscular Disorders Program at Stanford University. They did a lot of research on my particular form of muscular dystrophy. I attended the program's annual conference in January, where I met with several of the leading scientists and clinicians involved with myotonic dystrophy, including Dr. John Day, the first physician to discover the DM2 gene and a pioneer in the field. I had the opportunity to speak with patients and physicians about my own experience with the disease, its impact on me, and my plans to hike Mount Everest.

The encouragement I got from this group kept my adrenaline pumping. They helped me to see that I wasn't crazy or trying to achieve the impossible—and that if I could hike Mount Everest, I would inspire others to challenge themselves as well. That's what I wanted to do in climbing the mountain. I wanted to show others in my situation that their futures were not dark, that their limits were never as great as their potential.

I was so worked up with excitement after the conference that when I learned a blizzard in Chicago had closed the airports, I wasn't too disappointed that my flight was canceled. Once again, the unplanned detour turned into an opportunity: I extended my trip in California and went to San Diego to visit a close college friend and his family.

I wanted to keep up with my training while I was in San Diego, so I scaled the highest peak in town, Cowles Mountain. It stands a mere 1,593 feet above sea level, but if each foot is compared to a step on a staircase, that's a decent ascent—and it's a great place to go for a hike, too. Once I reached the top, I had the gift of a 360-degree view of the city. *What could be better?* I thought as I inhaled the mountain air. I couldn't smell it because of my anosmia, true, but I could feel it swirl through my lungs like a magical medicine that would one day make it possible for me to climb the Himalayas.

I followed my hike up Cowles Mountain with a trip to Black's Beach, the largest clothing-optional beach in the country, and one of the most famous in the world. I had traveled to San Diego a lot through the years but had never been to Black's Beach, so in my continued pursuit of bucket list items, I went.

Black's Beach is three hundred feet below the bluffs of Torrey Pines, and you have to go down a huge staircase to get there. After walking down to the beach, I walked and jogged for several miles. It was pretty secluded and there weren't many people there. I enjoyed the quiet beauty of the spectacular scenery—in a comfortable pair of running shorts and shoes. I wasn't about to jog naked and not protect my package.

By the time I returned to Chicago, I was definitely in the best shape I'd been in in years. Unfortunately, once back, I noticed a large lump in my arm that was getting bigger and hurt quite a bit whenever I bumped or touched it.

Over the years, I'd had lipomas, buildups of fatty tissue under the skin. However, they usually are not painful or anything to worry about. The first time I noticed them, there were several in my lower back and I was suffering a great deal of back pain. My physicians thought they were deep and large enough to potentially be pressing up against my nerve and recommended having them removed. Fortunately, they were benign, but there was no way to know if they were contributing to some of the intense back pain I'd suffered since breaking my back in high school.

Given that history, I wasn't overly concerned about the lumps on my arm, but I did my due diligence and followed up with a doctor to have it checked out.

All this work to get my body in shape, and I end up with a tumor that kills me, I thought, laughing to myself, as I probed the ugly lump in my right forearm that had grown to be the size of a golf ball. I imagined myself having to endure chemo on top of everything else. The irony wasn't lost on me.

"I don't know, Rob," my doctor said, taking a look at it. "This is larger than I'd like, and lipomas don't usually cause pain like this."

"I've had them before and the ones in my back caused a lot of pain," I said.

"Yes, but we don't know if that was because they were so close to your spinal cord and pressing up against your nerve. This one's in a pretty common spot and shouldn't be causing pain; we need to check it out."

"All right, but can't it wait?" I asked. "I'm in the midst of my training regimen to prepare for hiking Mount Everest in April. Can't it wait until my return?"

"No, Rob, I'm afraid it can't. Absolutely not! It could be more extensive than we can see here. We've got to remove it and do a biopsy as soon as we can to make sure it doesn't turn into a much bigger problem."

Once again, the limits of my body were testing the limits of my mind. How much more of this crap would I have to go through before I could head to Nepal?

The surgery was scheduled for early February, and as I waited, the pain grew greater, limiting my workouts. Once the surgery was over and the fatty tissue was established as nothing more than that—fatty tissue—I started physical therapy to help regain strength and range of motion in my arm. As soon as I was able, I was back at it with my cardiovascular training to prepare for Nepal.

By that point, I wasn't focusing so much on whether or not I could climb to Everest Base Camp. If Chris, who isn't a particularly active person, could do it, surely I could too. She'd joined me on a few hikes and complimented my conditioning. "Robby," she would say, catching her breath as I readied for more of a workout, "you're going to be in way better shape than anybody in my group was when I went!"

That kind of feedback kept me going—it gave me the confidence I needed. Still, I knew I could never risk being overly confident; problems always could arise.

Even though I like to be in control, one thing I've learned from all my health problems—and this was reinforced by my trip to Colorado—is that there are certain things you can't control. *If altitude sickness comes up, it is what it is,* I figured. *I will take my medicine; I will do everything within my control to properly prepare for the trip.* If something I couldn't have prepared for should happen, so be it.

Chris, ever the concerned nurse, cautioned me about my health.

"You still need to be careful, Robby. I worry about you going there with your health problems."

"Then I guess you'll have to join me, to keep an eye out for me," I said, smiling.

"No way! I'm not doing that again; once is enough!" she said, shaking her head vigorously.

The truth was, Chris had planned to join me from the beginning, but after doing the trek, she'd come home with no desire to do it again.

"No, Robby," she said again, "you have no idea how hard it is."

I could tell her resolve was weakening. "Do you want me to go alone?" I asked. "Is that what you're saying?"

Despite her protests, my sister loved adventure and was deeply concerned about me having medical issues at high altitude. So, after a long pause, she finally said, "All right, I'll go with you—just to be sure you're okay!"

So it was decided. Chris would join me for a hike up Mount Everest in April of 2015. What better way to convince my physicians that I would be all right than to take a trauma nurse along?

CHAPTER 15:

A BUMP IN THE ROAD

Nothing can stop the man with the right mental attitude from achieving his goal; nothing on earth can help the man with the wrong mental attitude.

—Thomas Jefferson

Chris wasn't the only one I wanted to join me on the trip. In the year that I'd been training for Everest, I'd imagined the trip so many times that it sometimes felt as if I'd already done it. In my imaginings, Chris and I were never alone. I imagined a whole team joining us—doctors, nurses, friends, and anyone who supported the idea of testing the limits of disability. If I could climb to Base Camp despite muscular dystrophy, a pacemaker, and a defibrillator that could shock my heart at any moment, then what could others with various health problems achieve? I wanted the trip to be about something more than just me climbing the mountain; I wanted it to be about going beyond our limits, about challenging the idea that a chronic, degenerative disease means that life and adventure must come to an end. What better way to demonstrate that purpose than to have a team of healthcare professionals behind me?

So my sister and I set out to put together a team of ten to twelve people, which is the ideal amount of passengers and equipment, given space and weight restrictions, for the flight from Kathmandu to Lukla, Nepal, where our trek would officially begin. (While Mount Everest does also border the south of Tibet, most climbers hike up the Nepal side since it is more popular for summit attempts and fewer trekking permits are required.)

What I thought would be a simple task of finding a team of physicians, nurses, and friends to join us, however, turned out to be impossible. No one wanted to make that kind of commitment—and a commitment it was! Timewise, the trip would last approximately three weeks, including two days of travel to Nepal, eight to twelve days of mountain ascent to Base Camp (depending on weather, conditioning, and pace), and another four or five days to descend back down the mountain before a full day of travel back to the United States.

Moneywise, the overall expense was roughly $3,500, which covered $2,300 for the porter and guides, all lodging and meals, the necessary permits, ground transportation, and local airfare in Nepal, and an estimated $1,200 for international airfare for a round-trip flight from Chicago to Kathmandu. This breakdown does not include the cost of equipment—hiking poles, shoes, a backpack, non-cotton clothing, a sleeping bag—which varies per individual.

Finally, anyone joining our team would also need to be active and healthy, with the ability to sustain multiple hours of continuous hiking at various grades in high altitude.

None of the physicians, nurses, or friends Chris and I asked had the combination of time, money, physical stamina, and interest to come along. The team concept didn't seem like it was going to happen. It would just be me and my sister.

Then, just as I was getting all the loose ends tied up, I invited a new friend who also loved to travel to come along. Kendra was in great shape, had hiked Mount Kilimanjaro, loved adventure, and had a well-paying job that included a very flexible schedule.

"Hey, why don't you join us!" I suggested.

After discussing some details of the trip, she said, "Sure! Let's do it!" Just like that, as if I'd suggested we go out for a movie sometime.

I thought she'd be the perfect travel companion. We got along well, she had traveled a lot on her own, and I was confident she'd be a good hiking partner, so our team of two became three.

Next, since every team needs an identity, we thought of a name for our trek. Based on our ambitions and goals, along with the potential future title of my book (yes, writing about my recovery was always a goal of mine!), our journey became known as For Ever Strong. The name originated from a play on words: I would be forty (For) years old while we were doing the hiking expedition to the base camp of Mount Everest (Ever), and I wanted to encourage people to remain "Strong" throughout life's trials and tribulations.

Logistics proved to be fairly easy, since Chris had done the hike before. We were able to book the trip with the same expedition service she'd used the first time, a company in Nepal called Shangri-La Nepal Trek.

The guy who owned the company, Jiban, was in his late forties and had a wealth of knowledge and experience. He was also familiar with some of the potential obstacles that stood in our way since he was already familiar with my medical history and knew that I had tried to join my sister on the expedition in 2013. He took care of arranging for all our hotels, lodging, and meals for the trip, as well as two guides and a porter to support us and help carry our gear along the way. All we had to do was get there.

The question of when to go wasn't a tough one; there are only a few months out of the year when it is possible to make the climb to Base Camp, and April is considered best because it's the beginning of the hiking season, before the mountains are overly crowded. We didn't finalize the exact dates until the last minute, however, and—just as I'd found with my trip to Colorado—I would come to discover later in the Mount Everest trip that a small adjustment that seems insignificant at the time can sometimes end up being the difference between life and death.

When it came to specifics, there were a couple of things that influenced our timeline. Thinking I might never get to that side of the world again, it seemed like the perfect opportunity to visit India, which borders Nepal, and see the Taj Mahal. I'd seen the pyramids in Egypt and the Great Wall in China, and now I wanted to see an architectural marvel like the Taj Mahal, a marble mausoleum the Mughal emperor Shah

Jahan commissioned to be built for his deceased wife, Mumtaz Mahal, in the seventeenth century.

Of course, I had to schedule the flight so I could make it to the Cubs' 2015 home opener at Wrigley Field the night before, too. And since I'm a glutton for punishment, I took another factor into consideration when planning the trip: I wanted to run the Disney Expedition Everest Challenge, a 5K event with obstacles, on my way back from Mount Everest. Now, I know it might seem a bit silly wanting to run a Disney race called Expedition Everest when I was going to be doing the real thing, but for me, the training, commitment, and achievement of reaching Everest Base Camp was similar to preparing for the Olympics. I may have looked healthy and back to being in good shape, but inside I was ailing—I was a diseased man with so many health issues that the medications I took each and every day made my bedside table look like a pharmacy. I wanted something to mark my achievement—a memento symbolizing all the hard work and preparation I'd done in order to go on this adventure. Clearly, no one was going to drape a medal around my neck once I reached my goal in Nepal—but they would at the end of this race in Disney World!

In order for me to make it back in time for the May 2nd race in Orlando, the Mount Everest hike had to be in early April. So we set a departure date for April 6th, with an arrival in India on April 7th. We'd tour India until the 10th and then fly to Kathmandu to begin our trek on April 12th.

Chris and I booked tickets for the same flight on Air India but, unfortunately, there was a mistake when Kendra purchased hers; since she wasn't flying direct to India, she would have to meet us in Delhi.

We knew we'd need visas to travel to India. When I contacted a travel agency, I was told we would not need to get them in advance, that once we got to Delhi, we could get them at the airport. That seemed odd, so I called Air India as well, and they assured me the travel agency was correct—we could get our travel visas in Delhi upon arrival. Everything was set.

▲▲ ▲▲ ▲▲

On April 6th, with our tickets and passports in hand, Chris and I headed to Chicago's O'Hare International Airport.

I don't think I'd ever been so excited. I was forty years old and felt like a kid in a candy store. I could barely stand the anticipation. At long last, I was doing what everyone thought I could never do—climb the world's tallest mountain—with a heart that was pieced together with wires and electronics, and a neuromuscular system that might as well have been bought at a garage sale. All those years of setbacks, of constant health problems, of surgeries and recoveries; all those years of training and working out and pushing myself when all I really wanted to do was crawl into a hole and go to sleep. Now, finally, I was actually doing it!

Chris and I slowly moved through the check-in line, dragging our heavy gear, my heart beating with joy and enthusiasm. It's a wonder my defibrillator didn't go off, I was so excited!

When we reached the Air India ticket counter, I handed the agent my ticket and passport and said, "Here you go! One bag to check and one carry-on, and I made sure they were within regulation. You have no idea how long I've been planning this trip!"

"Your visa?" the agent asked.

"I'll get that in Delhi," I said confidently.

"I'm sorry, but you must have your visa in order to board the plane."

My heart sank to the floor. "What do you mean?" I asked. "I was assured I could get it in Delhi upon our arrival."

"Here's mine," Chris interjected, having gotten hers in advance.

Chris was perturbed that I had not obtained my visa already as well, and she made it clear that she wasn't going to wait for me; the agent quickly processed her visa and turned back to me.

"I don't know who told you that, but we can't let you go to India without a visa."

"I looked it up online. Then I called a travel agent and also called Air India to confirm. Everyone I spoke with said I could get a travel visa on arrival for such a short stay."

"They didn't tell you accurately," she said. "You'll have to get one from the Indian embassy and return tomorrow."

I was shocked and outraged. They had to let us on the flight.

Unfortunately, no matter how much I protested and pleaded, and no matter how many frantic, last-minute calls I made to the travel agency and Indian embassy, the agent was adamant. She simply wasn't going to let me on the flight.

Chris received her boarding pass, gave me a hug, and left for her flight. She wasn't about to let my mishap get in the way of her travel.

As for me, there was no way I could get to the Indian embassy and get a visa approved on such short notice, so the only thing to do was go home and book a flight straight to Nepal. I would have to kiss the possibility of visiting India and the Taj Mahal on this trip good-bye.

I felt as if Christmas had come and Santa had passed me by. I wanted to sob to the heavens, I was so upset.

If this is a sign of what's up ahead, it's going to be a disaster, I thought.

After returning home from the airport, I quickly got myself under control. I took out my rage with a mix of push-ups, sit-ups, curls, and a few rounds on my punching bag, and then I hit the phones to begin making alternate arrangements for travel the following day.

That's when I discovered that the airline could have sent me to India on the same flight as my sister and simply not allowed me to leave the airport. Then they could have rebooked my flight from India to Nepal so I could head there the following day instead of several days later, as we'd originally booked it.

Discovering how unnecessary it had been for the agents at the airport to send me back home made me even more angry than I already was. Nevertheless, I realized how pointless it would be to dwell on my anger, so instead I decided to take a nap. I was going to miss the Taj Mahal, true, but I wasn't going to miss out on fulfilling my goal. Just one more day and I'd be on a jet heading for Kathmandu. *I've waited this long,* I told myself. *I only need to make it through one more night, then I'll be on my way.* This was just one more detour on the road of obstacles I'd had to overcome to get this far.

As I slowly fell asleep, a sudden peace overcame me. The frantic travel days in India were being eliminated. I could relax and concentrate on Mount Everest.

Eighteen days later, I would discover that missing my flight was one detour that helped save my life.

CHAPTER 16:

WELCOME TO NEPAL

He who is not courageous enough to take risks will accomplish nothing in life.

—Muhammad Ali

When I arrived at O'Hare International Airport the next morning, I told the agent at the counter what had happened the previous day and what I'd learned after I was sent home.

"Yes, you're right," she said. "You could have traveled on the same flight to Delhi and rebooked the connection to Kathmandu."

"Well, why didn't they tell me that yesterday?" I asked. "I could have been on the flight with my sister."

"I don't know why you were told that," she said, "but don't worry, we'll get you on a new flight today."

I was relieved and thanked her for her assistance. She was much nicer than the agent I'd encountered the day before.

"That will be $600," she added. "There'll be a $400 fee for changing the ticket, and another $200 for the flight from Delhi to Kathmandu."

"What?!" I said. "I shouldn't have to pay for a mistake by your agent. I should have been on the flight to Delhi yesterday."

"Yes, but this is a different flight. You'll have to pay for a new ticket."

The pleasant agent grew far less pleasant, as did I, and after we went round and round about the cost of the ticket, I became so frustrated, I finally left and walked over to another airline to review my options. Etihad Airlines had a flight leaving around the same time, and with an earlier connection to Kathmandu. I would get there a day earlier, and the new ticket was only $650. It was a no-brainer. I purchased that ticket and was on my way. Operation For Ever Strong had begun!

After a layover in Abu Dhabi, I landed in Kathmandu at nine o'clock the following evening, ten hours and forty-five minutes later than Chicago time. Here's an interesting, fun fact: Nepal Standard Time is one of only three time zones in the world that has a forty-five-minute offset from Coordinated Universal Time, the primary standard by which the world regulates its clocks and time. (The others are Chatham Standard Time and the unofficial Australian Central Western Time.)

When I got off the plane, I was hoping to see Chris's familiar face. Since I wasn't joining her in India, she had changed her ticket in Delhi and had already arrived in Kathmandu. But I didn't see her at the airport; instead, I saw a well-groomed, good-looking guy of average height and build—Jiban, our trip organizer. He and I recognized each other immediately, both from Facebook photos and from a breakfast we'd had in New York almost a year earlier when we both happened be in the Big Apple at the same time. Chris, who knew Jiban from her first Mount Everest trip, had made the introduction.

"Hi, Rob," Jiban said, "it's nice to see you again. How was your flight? I heard you had some trouble with the visas." He had a warm smile that matched the warmth of his personality, and I liked him from the beginning.

Jiban drove me through Kathmandu in his nice Ford pickup truck. Unfortunately, I couldn't see much; it was dark out, and there were few lights during many stretches of the bumpy drive. From what little I could discern, Kathmandu appeared to be a fairly compact city, and a chaotic one at that. As we neared the city center, horns tooted, drivers shouted, and mopeds swarmed around us like motorized mosquitoes. There wasn't a single stop sign or traffic light to put some order to the chaos. That didn't seem to faze Jiban in the slightest; he just wove in and out of the traffic with the elegance of a trained dancer while I wondered in amazement with every passing car how he managed to keep his truck dent-free.

Jiban brought me straight to Hotel Yak & Yeti, a beautiful, five-star hotel that was lit up like the Taj Mahal I'd so unfortunately had to miss. (Yes, still a proverbial thorn in my side.) After checking in at the front desk, I walked over to the hotel bar, where I saw Chris hanging out and having a drink. After dropping my luggage in my room, I joined her and Jiban back at the bar. I drank a beer called Everest before heading back up to my room, where I fell into a very deep, much-needed sleep.

▲▲ ▲▲ ▲▲

When I woke up the next morning I was still exhausted, but my excitement won out. I was eager to start the day. Kendra, who had spent her first night in a hostel, joined me, Chris, and Jiban for breakfast in the hotel. At last, our For Ever Strong team was all together, and our adventure was about to begin!

Given our two-day-early arrival in Kathmandu, Jiban suggested we spend one day exploring the city before catching a flight to Lukla the following morning. Lukla, a central location in the Khumbu region of the Himalayas, is the main staging area in the mountains for trekkers and climbers to begin their journey. This was where our hike to Everest Base Camp officially would commence.

After breakfast, Jiban had to tend to other guests, leaving my sister, Kendra, and me to explore Kathmandu on our own.

"Hey, Rob, check that out," Chris said, nodding to an array of colorful banners that had been affixed to the fence just outside the Yak & Yeti that were for climbing teams staying at the hotel. I gave them a quick glance but was too absorbed by the sights and sounds that surrounded us as we began to wander through the amazing Himalayan city to pay them much attention.

Kathmandu, one of the fastest-growing South Asian cities, is two thousand years old and lies in the center of the Kathmandu Valley, 4,600 feet above sea level. It's a rambling city with hundreds of thousands of four-, five-, and six-story rectangular buildings spread across a valley wreathed by spectacular mountains. Over half a million people live in Kathmandu, and I swear almost every one of them was in the street—walking, peddling merchandise, and zipping by on mopeds—while we were touring. Mopeds were everywhere, honking and moving in and out of the chaotic traffic of buses, taxis, and private cars. The air was thick with pollution from the vehicles, so I wasn't surprised by all the people wearing black face masks over their noses and mouths. In fact, according to a study by Yale University, Nepal's air quality is the fourth worst in the world due to the high number of vehicles on the road and construction projects going on.

We walked through the dusty, crowded streets and took in the sights. There were open-air markets with everything from hardware to bright, colorful scarves and clothes stacked high and hanging like banners. Police rode around on bicycles, cows slept in the road, and scrawny, mangy dogs lay about or wandered around, looking for bits of garbage to eat.

Perhaps what struck me the most, however, was what we saw when we reached the main road: a Kentucky Fried Chicken and Pizza Hut. They looked completely out of place. We had a good laugh and vowed not to eat there during our trip.

There was also a ton of construction. It seemed that on every block there was a rubble of concrete and building supplies, suggesting something was in some stage of construction, but many of the projects seemed to have been abandoned. I wondered if there was no money available to finish them. That, plus the heavy dust in the air, contributed to the sense of disarray.

Most of what I felt was a sense of awe and wonder at how much life was swarming all around us. Whole families spilled out of tiny homes that weren't much more than ridged metal sheds, while sellers melodically cried out, announcing the products they had for sale. Everywhere there were people, and everywhere there were smiles. I felt so happy to be among them.

"I need to get a SIM card for my phone," Chris said, "and we should find a pharmacy to pick up some antibiotics."

"We should get some antidiarrheal too, just in case," added Kendra, who had done a lot of traveling in developing countries.

Our first stop was at a mobile store, where we asked an employee for directions to a pharmacy. In broken English, the man explained where we had to go. As we navigated the streets, we hoped we understood the directions he'd given us.

"There's one," Chris said, pointing to a shack filled with stacks upon stacks of colorful boxes.

"One what?" I asked, bewildered.

"A pharmacy," she said.

It looked more like a tiny newsstand. We approached the kiosk and the woman inside fortunately spoke a bit of English. We explained what we wanted, and she dug through what seemed to be a disorganized mess. Despite the chaos, she quickly found what she was looking for, then handed over a couple packs of pills in foil packets. They weren't in sealed boxes or anything, and there were no questions asked about prescriptions. We all bought a pack of the antidiarrheal Eldoper.

Purchases in hand, we headed back to the hotel to meet up with Jiban for lunch.

"Those banners are so pretty," Chris reiterated as we passed by them again on the way into the hotel. I agreed, too weary to spend much time enjoying the bright display. All I wanted to do was have lunch and hopefully take a nap.

▲▲ ▲▲ ▲▲

Lunch was a delicious, buffet-style meal of *dal bhat*, sort of a rice and lentil soup served with more rice and curried vegetables. It was really good, and just what I needed to feel recharged and happy. I was beat when we sat down to eat, but just talking to Jiban about our itinerary got me all excited again to start the climb the following morning.

"In preparation for tomorrow, we'll do a gear check," Jiban told us. "I'll be coming to your rooms this afternoon at four to make sure you've got everything you need. The weight of your pack is very important, so don't bring anything you don't need up there. At the same time, you don't want to find out halfway up the mountain that you've forgotten anything. You need to have weatherproof clothing and avoid anything with cotton—it will absorb any moisture in the air, along with your sweat, and it takes forever to dry. In the cold air, it can freeze." He looked at each of us closely. "Cotton can kill you on the mountain, so I want to be sure you don't have any."

We assured Jiban we would pack carefully, and then Kendra and I said good-bye to Chris and Jiban and headed back to the hotel room we were sharing to spend the afternoon going over our gear. Chris had already done her gear check with Jiban the day before.

"All right, let's get this done," I said.

By the time we finished laying out all of our different pieces on the bed for Jiban to review, I'd realized taking that much-needed nap was clearly out of the question. Since we had to be prepared for two weeks in the mountains and be ready for anything and everything, including rain, ice, snow, and sun, both beds were completely covered with various articles of clothing, toiletries, and equipment, leaving no place to lie down.

When Jiban and Chris arrived, we spent the next hour going over our gear, which included a couple pairs of trekking pants, waterproof jackets and pants, insulated pants, two pairs of gloves and socks, hiking boots, slippers for walking around the tea houses, long underwear, hats, long-sleeved shirts, short-sleeved shirts, water bottles, trekking poles, first aid kits, sunscreen, water purification tablets, and toilet paper. All the clothing was lightweight and would dry quickly if it got wet.

Somehow, we had to force it all into our duffel bag. We did have some relief, though: We'd have a porter who would come and get our duffel bags from our rooms each morning of the hike and take them to our next night's stop for us. All we'd have to carry were our day packs, filled with anything we might need during the day. Not knowing the weather conditions and ascending to different elevations each day meant we had to be prepared with warm, weatherproof clothing, water, and whatever snacks we might want, even in our small day packs.

After all our gear was laid out, checked, double-checked, and triple-checked, Jiban came by and checked it all again. After he was finished, we packed it all back into our hiking packs and duffel bags so we could be ready for the morning flight.

"Ugh! Robby, your pack is too heavy!" Chris said as she weighed our bags with a portable bag scale she had brought for this very reason. "You're going to be overweight on the flight."

"I know it's heavy," I said, "but I have less equipment than you have. Since I'm bigger, my clothes are bigger and heavier. I don't know if my bag can get much lighter!"

"Don't worry about it," Jiban interjected. "I will take care of it. That reminds me, Rob, the porter will carry a canister of oxygen for you in case you have any problems at altitude."

Jiban was great. All throughout the trip, he was on top of things, always anticipating our needs, alleviating a tremendous amount of stress.

"Why don't you guys take a break," he suggested. He was busy helping other guests prepare for their own treks, including a Chilean expedition team that would be on our flight over to Lukla the next day.

Kendra, Chris, and I went back outside the hotel to take pictures, and once again, Chris pointed out how colorful the banners were.

"Yeah, I know," I told her, wondering why she was so insistent on pointing them out.

Chris sighed, and she and Kendra practically walked me over to the fence to look at them more closely.

"Check it out," Kendra said in a tone that made it clear there was something she wanted me to see.

That's when I saw it. Amongst all the banners hung for the various hiking teams, there was a big blue and green one that read:

Welcome to
FOR EVER STRONG—Everest Base Camp Trek—Spring 2015

"Jiban had the banner made especially for you," Kendra said.

"Oh," I said, stunned. "Wow! That is just awesome! I don't know how I could have missed it!"

"I know, Rob," Chris said. "We've been trying to get you to notice all day!"

"Yeah, I guess," I said, still smiling at the amazing banner.

When Jiban came outside a short while later, I walked over to give him a hug. "Thank you so much!" I said.

"You're very welcome," he replied, smiling at my contentment.

After taking several pictures with the banners, we headed back inside to enjoy some time on the fifth floor, where there was a special

VIP area where we could sit, have some drinks and hors d'oeuvres, and finalize our plans for the next day.

Kendra and I were exhausted later that evening, so we decided to skip a nine o'clock dinner with the Chilean team and headed back to the room, where we ordered room service and collapsed into bed.

I had no idea how I'd get the energy to climb a mountain, but one way or another, I'd better find it fast.

From the moment we stepped off the plane in Lukla and throughout the entire hike up to Everest Base Camp, colorful prayer flags put up by the Nepali people surrounded us everywhere we looked.

With the help of Chris (left) and Kendra (center), I was able to quickly get over my fear of heights and cross the countless bridges we had to traverse throughout our journey in the Himalayas.

Many yaks carrying heavy loads are guided along the mountain trails, forcing hikers to stay close to the mountain or risk getting pushed off the side and falling to their demise.

The scenery of Sagarmatha trail is majestic, but no, that isn't Mount Everest behind me. It would be several more days after this photo was taken before I would lay eyes on the world's tallest mountain.

I was amazed by the superhuman strength of the Sherpas, who showed little sign of fatigue while carrying heavy loads to remote villages. I even considered jumping on one of their tall stacks for a piggyback ride up the mountain.

My doctors and I were concerned about how my medical conditions might be affected by the high elevations, but in the end it was my sister who suffered altitude sickness and needed to be medically evacuated before reaching Base Camp.

Reaching Mount Everest Base Camp in front of Khumbu Icefall was more than I could have hoped as I celebrated the achievement with my guides, Kendra, and the Chilean Expedition Team. Pictured (from left) are: Babu, Kendra, Rodrigo Lara Fernandez, myself, Chilean photographer Fernando Borquez, Kumar, and famous Chilean climber Ernesto Olivares Miranda.

Meeting famous Nepali Sherpa mountain climber Jamling Tenzing Norgay on my return from Base Camp was a perfect storybook ending to the trip. He is the son of Tenzing Norgay, who, along with Sir Edmund Hillary, was the first to summit Mount Everest on May 26, 1953.

Upon our safe return to Lukla on April 24, 2015, our trekking team (from left)—Babu, myself, Kendra, our porter for the trip, and Kumar—enjoyed celebratory drinks of Everest Beer and whiskey.

I was lucky to survive the 7.8-magnitude earthquake that struck Nepal the afternoon of April 25, 2015. The event was devastating to the region, destroying thousands of homes and many villages, forcing survivors to search for victims among the mounds of rubble and debris.

The day after the earthquake, we were evacuated from Lukla on an emergency helicopter. When we landed in Kathmandu, we learned that a 6.7-magnitude aftershock had struck the region while we were still in the air.

After returning safely back to Chicago in May 2015, I was invited to deliver the game ball and rosin bag to the pitcher's mound before a game between the Cubs and Dodgers. Then, a year later, thanks to season ticket representative Frank Cascella and the Cubs, I was able to live a dream and throw out a ceremonial first pitch at Wrigley Field on April 26, 2016, almost two years to the day after the devastating earthquake in Nepal.

PART III

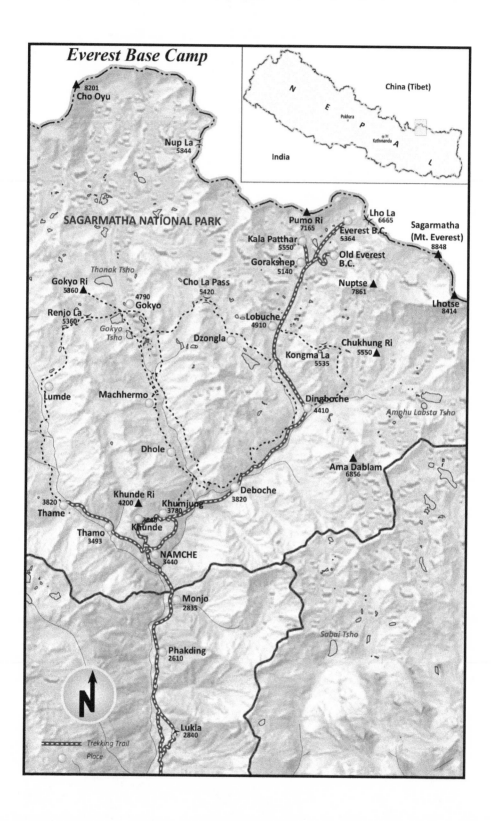

CHAPTER 17:

THE JOURNEY BEGINS

The secret of getting ahead is getting started.

—Mark Twain

We were originally scheduled to fly from Kathmandu into Lukla, where our hike to Everest Base Camp would commence, on April 12th. However, since we arrived in Nepal earlier than planned, we pushed our trip forward by two days so we wouldn't be pressed for time. That decision, it turned out, was a fateful one.

The morning of our flight to Lukla, a small town in eastern Nepal about 9,300 feet above sea level, I was still exhausted but extremely excited. By that point, I had been going back and forth between being tired and excited so frequently that the two feelings had begun to blur.

Jiban met us at 6:00 a.m. As we waited outside the hotel for the bus that would take us to the airport, Jiban introduced me to the three men who made up the Chilean Everest and Lhotse Expedition Team. Their team was headed by Ernesto Olivares Miranda, a man of about fifty who had summited Mount Everest before. His partner for the climb was a gentleman by the name of Rodrigo, and they had brought a photographer named Fernando along. The trio planned to not only reach the summit of Mount Everest but to also become the first Chilean expedition team to traverse the South Col—a sharp-edged pass located on the Nepal side of Mount Everest that sits between Mount Everest and Mount Lhotse—and also climb Mount Lhotse, which has the second-tallest peak in the area and is the fourth-highest mountain in the world. I enjoyed chatting with them and telling them about my trip to Chile back when Chris and I went to Antarctica.

The bus finally reached a small domestic airport in Kathmandu that looked more like an abandoned warehouse under construction. It was a nightmare. There was construction all over and only one door to get into the building with a bunch of people chaotically trying to push their way through. Just like the streets, which had no stop lights or lanes, there were no lines or organization at all—it was crazy.

"Don't worry," Jiban said when I asked about the chaos. "Nepal is not a very organized country; you'll get used to it."

"Okay, if you say so," I said, laughing. I figured if he wasn't worried about it, I wasn't going to sweat it either.

After about an hour of inching forward through the crowd, we finally squeezed through the door. Once inside the airport, I realized he was right. It was perfectly fine inside.

As Jiban took care of business and got us situated for our flights, Kendra, Chris, and I discussed concerns about our luggage being overweight. There were signs posted indicating strict weight limits for checked luggage on the plane. If we exceeded them, they said, we wouldn't be able to board. After the fiasco at O'Hare, I didn't want to take any chances.

"Jiban," I said when he returned, "our bags might be too heavy."

"Don't worry, you'll be fine," he said, dismissing the concern.

"Are you sure?" Chris asked. "He's over the weight limit."

He waved his hand. "I'll take care of it, don't worry."

Sure enough, our tickets and our bags were all accepted without any problem. I'm not exactly sure how he did it, but Jiban seemed like the Godfather of Nepal. Everyone knew him and he knew how to get things done.

Jiban would not be accompanying us on the hike itself. Instead, we had two guides: Babu, who would meet us when we arrived in Lukla, and Kumar, who had just joined us at the airport in Kathmandu.

When we said our good-byes to Jiban, I felt a little nervous. I'd come to rely on him over the past couple of days. Kumar noticed my unease.

"Don't worry, Rob, sir," he said, smiling broadly. "We take care of you."

He wasn't big, but he had an athletic build and was a real charmer. He sported an earring and had a cool-guy sort of vibe. Chris and Kendra immediately took to him. I found him to be a good guy, young and vibrant and full of confidence—the right personality to lead us on our journey.

We walked outside and boarded buses that took us straight to the tarmac, where our plane was waiting. It was a little twin-engine propeller plane that looked to be ancient and like it was probably held together with duct tape.

Getting on the plane was the real deal—no turning back now! We all squeezed into the tiny aircraft, which had only one row of seats on the left side and two adjoining seats on the right side. I took two seats near the back of the plane: one for myself and the other to rest our three day packs on. There were two pilots up front and the door to their cabin was open so we could watch out the front window throughout the flight.

As the plane took off, rattling through the sky for the forty-five-minute flight to Lukla, a flight attendant appeared and began handing out candy and cotton balls. I thought it was strange enough to have a flight attendant on such a small flight, but I found the candy and cotton balls even stranger, so I declined them.

"You'd better take them," Rodrigo suggested, shouting over the roar of the engine. "They'll keep your ears from popping!" Then he demonstrated by putting the cotton balls in his ears. Then I realized that sucking on the candy was like chewing gum and also would help keep our ears from popping.

"Oh, yeah, okay," I said and caught the attention of the flight attendant so I could get some.

We hadn't been in the air very long before all I could say was "wow" and "wow" again and again. The scenery was amazing, absolutely beautiful. There were mountains on both sides of us. At times they looked so close, it seemed like we could open our windows and touch the nearby trees, a sea of green leading up to snowy mountain peaks in the distance.

April is the hottest time of the year in the Himalayas, with temperatures sometimes reaching upward of 80 degrees during the day. The permanent snow line, the point above which snow and ice cover the ground year-round, is about 18,700 feet above sea level, more than a thousand feet higher than Base Camp.

As we swooped lower and closer to the mountains, iridescent-green, terraced rice fields, colorful rooftops, and splashes of pink from the blooming rhododendrons cast a magical quality to the secluded world we were flying into.

I could certainly understand some people being fearful in such a situation, but in my travels, I've flown on enough prop planes that I've come to trust them. Besides, this plane was old, and it hadn't gotten that way by crashing. It had clearly survived thousands, maybe even tens of thousands, of flights and I was pretty sure it would survive this one, too.

What was more frightening than the aircraft itself was the airport we'd be landing at. Not only is the Lukla airport one of the smallest airports in the world, it's also considered one of the most dangerous. As we approached, I understood why.

Flying so high in the mountains, there didn't seem to be much of a descent. The only reason we knew we were landing was by the sound of the landing gear engaging. The tiny landing strip came into view through the front windshield of the plane, and it seemed to slash right through the village, with houses alongside it. It wasn't a flat landing strip; it had an uphill slant, meaning the plane had to land at just the right angle. Straight ahead was a massive mountain, and on the other side a massive but narrow drop-off.

The minute our wheels touched the runway and we began speeding straight toward the mountain, I was captivated by how quickly the pilots were able to stop the plane before crashing into the rocks ahead.

I gripped the arms of the seat tightly and watched as we sped straight toward the mountain, stopping just meters before the end of the runway. Immediately, there was an eruption of applause and cheers at our successful landing. I was impressed at how the pilots took the whole landing in stride; they just turned and smiled back at us, clearly accustomed to the reaction foreigners had to such a risky landing. For them, it was just another day at work.

Once we got off the plane, I was all set to start hiking. As I was beginning to learn, however, in Nepal, everything is relaxed. This stop in Lukla would prove to be no different.

First, we were greeted by Babu, our other guide. Babu was young and thin with a cute-boy image; he appeared like he had just finished high school. He spoke limited English, but Kumar spoke enough that we could still communicate well. They suggested we join the Chilean team for tea before beginning our trek.

I wanted to get started so badly, all I could think about was hitting the trail. I didn't want to stop for tea and I didn't want to go sightseeing. I wanted to hike in the Himalayas. And frankly, I was afraid if I did rest, I'd lose my energy to continue. I was still jet-lagged from the trans-Atlantic flight, and my medications have always affected my energy level. If I sat down, I feared I'd never want to get up and get going.

My having that kind of attitude wasn't going to get us anywhere, though, so I begrudgingly accepted that the morning would be slow getting started. After we finished our tea, it was clear our guides were still in no hurry, so after rearranging our packs so our porter could move on without us, we took a walk through town, enjoying the curious children, who watched us as if we were aliens from outer space, and the not-so-curious adults, who either acted like we were invisible, smiled and called for us to buy something from them, or just warily checked us out as we walked by.

Walking through the town, I kind of felt like a cool American. It was obvious what we were there to do. To the residents of Lukla, though, we were just another set of tourists. They were not overly impressed, and cool as I felt I was, I clearly wasn't special in their eyes.

The Nepalese certainly like visitors coming in, as the number one source of income in Nepal is tourism. However, because there are many reports about Westerners leaving garbage along the Himalayan trails, there is also a feeling of resentment toward them.

Instead of worrying about their impressions of me, however, I needed to focus on the positive. With each and every step of the way, I began to appreciate the magnitude of what we were about to do. It was a "holy cow" moment—something I'd been planning for two years was finally going to happen! I was so eager to hit the trail, I felt like a racehorse who'd been locked in the starting gate: I was desperate for the gate to open.

Instead, we went shopping. Well, more like window shopping. Even in such a remote place, there was pretty much everything to buy. There were internet cafés, gear shops, and, believe it or not, a Starbucks.

As we continued walking through town, we reached a memorial gate dedicated to Pasang Lhamu Sherpa, a Nepalese national hero who was the first Sherpa woman to summit Mount Everest, in 1993. Passing underneath the arch symbolizing her accomplishment, we began our trek to Everest Base Camp.

"Where is it?" I asked.

"Where is what, Rob, sir?" Kumar responded.

"Mount Everest," I clarified.

"Oh, you see in few days," Kumar explained, which really surprised me. I was flabbergasted we couldn't already see the tallest mountain in the world from where we were. What we could see, however, was unbelievable. The entire area was surrounded by incredibly beautiful mountains that rose into the sky as if they were growing taller by the minute. I'd been all over the world, but I had never seen anything as incredible as the enveloping embrace of the Himalaya mountains encircling us.

Hiking to Base Camp would take eight to twelve days and take us to 17,600 feet above sea level, more than 7,000 feet higher than my training in Alma.

The hike to Base Camp would take much longer than the hike down, not only because it's uphill but because we would have to acclimatize as we ascended. If you go too high too quickly, you'll get altitude sickness—the number one cause of death on Mount Everest. Altitude sickness is no joke: it means your body isn't getting enough oxygen. Your body needs to slowly adapt to the higher altitude by making more red blood cells to carry the oxygen to your brain.

Altitude sickness can cause nausea and severe headaches and delirium, and we were warned that if any of us got severe headaches, we would need to get to a lower elevation fast. We were still adjusting to the altitude, and all of us—even Chris, who'd had an extra day to rest in Kathmandu—were fatigued. So we knew we were going to have to acclimatize as we ascended.

There were other dangers as well. The trails could be narrow and crowded, and while people were pretty good about navigating around each other, we were warned about the yaks.

"When yaks on the trail, you get back," Kumar told us. "Step off trail and go uphill. Yaks will push you right off the mountain if you don't."

The rains will turn the dirt trail to slippery mud, and slipping can mean falling to your death. Even just a twisted ankle can make returning to Lukla difficult, and a broken bone can be disastrous.

There was no telling if or when we might encounter a natural disaster. Avalanches are common in the mountains, and blizzards, snowstorms, and torrential rainstorms were all possibilities. The hike ahead was dangerous for even the healthiest of hikers. For someone with a bad heart and muscular dystrophy like myself, there was no telling what could happen.

"You ready?" Chris asked me.

"Absolutely!" I answered. "You?"

"I feel like shit to be honest, but let's get going."

With that, Kumar and Babu led the way. The porter had already advanced on the trail ahead of us, showing no sign of weakness while carrying all three of our heavy bags of gear on his back.

Including the porter, six of us would be going uphill.

Only five of us would be hiking down.

CHAPTER 18:

MOUNTAINS AND VALLEYS

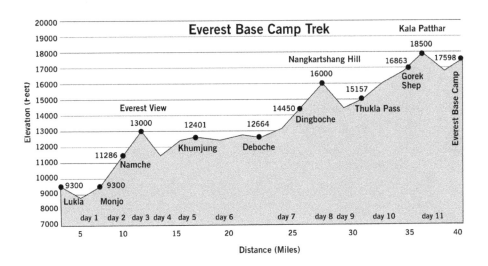

Believe you can and you're halfway there.

—Theodore Roosevelt

O ur first destination was Phakding, where we would be stopping for lunch. It would be about a three-hour hike, which didn't sound very long to me. I was anticipating five or six hours per day and knew if I stopped hiking after three hours, it would be hard for me to get up and go farther.

"Three hours and a break for lunch is good," Kumar said. "Take it easy on your first day."

"All right," I agreed, knowing from then on, Kumar was the one in charge.

The day couldn't have been nicer: it was not too hot and not too cool, and the sky was crystal clear. With our bad-weather gear stuffed away in our packs, we were perfectly comfortable wearing light pants and T-shirts.

However, I soon realized that my day pack was much heavier than it needed to be. I had been so concerned about not being prepared that I had overpacked. I had too many clothes, too many Clif bars, too many liters of water, too much unnecessary gear, a laptop computer, and my heart magnet. Though we were supposed to just be prepared for the weather, I was prepared for calamity, and my back was paying the price.

As we walked, we followed a path leading downward, which surprised me.

"This is weird," I said. "When do we start going uphill?"

"Oh, yeah," Chris said, "that was the part I didn't want to tell you about. We go downhill most of the way today."

"Why are we going downhill? That just seems like a waste of time!" I joked.

Chris and Kendra laughed.

"I was so frustrated when I did this before," Chris said. "Whatever time we spend going downhill, we have to make up for on the way back up."

Chris and I had talked several times before the trip about the changes in elevation and the need to acclimatize along the way. There were stages built into the trip to hike higher during the day and then sleep at a lower altitude during the night to help the body adjust to the changes in elevation and prevent altitude sickness.

"It's okay," Kumar said, "you be okay, Rob, sir. These are 'Nepali flats.'"

The Nepali people are so accustomed to the up-and-down terrain in the mountains, "uphill" might as well be "flat" to them. "Nepali flats" became the running joke for the remainder of our trip.

We all took a deep breath in preparation as we began our descent.

Phakding has an elevation of 8,563 feet, which is about 800 feet lower than Lukla. The descent felt weird, but like everything in life, sometimes you have to take a step backwards before you can begin to go forward. I had been an athlete long enough to understand that in training, you don't always feel as if you're making progress but if you continue, you reach a point where you realize that you'd been advancing all along. So that is how I decided to view the hike downhill, and I dedicated myself to simply enjoying the amazing experience.

We passed through several small villages, which were nothing more than a cluster of houses, small farming plots, and the occasional kiosk. Everywhere we turned, there were long rows of rectangular flags strung together. They looked like sheets of colorful paper that had been scribbled upon.

"They're prayer flags," Kumar explained, noting that the five different colors represent the five different elements. Blue symbolizes the sky and space; white, the air and wind; red, fire; green, water; and yellow, the earth.

"In traditional Tibetan medicine," Kumar continued, "the balance of these elements brings health and harmony. Each flag has a prayer written on it. When they flutter in the wind, the prayers are sent to heaven."

I liked that idea and felt it was just what we needed—to send off our prayers for a safe and successful hike.

The colorful prayer flags added a festive touch to the otherwise tranquil landscape. There were birds flying high overhead, as well as brown-and-grey Tibetan snowcocks that were hard to see at first because they blended into the background as they strutted around the ground like pigeons, pecking for food. They had these funny, loud, cackling cries; they startled me at first, but I soon got used to them.

As we hiked, occasionally going uphill and then back down, we soon fell into a routine with Babu in the lead, Kendra behind him, Chris and Kumar in the rear, and me in the middle. We each seemed to hike at our own pace and weren't really walking together. It worked well, giving me some solitude as I took in the fact that this trip was actually happening. For two years I had planned it and trained my body, and now I was grateful that I had. It was strenuous walking at such a high altitude, where it was difficult to breathe. I realized my doctors had been right to worry that my heart might not be able to take it. However, I felt good; I felt strong. I just had to keep a close check on my heart rate.

As Phakding came into view, we reached one of several bridges we would have to cross. They were really long, narrow swaying bridges that weren't much more than laced-together steel slats and long lengths of cyclone fencing on either side to keep hikers from plummeting to the raging rivers below.

"You guys are going to have to help me go over it," I told Chris and Kendra when we reached this particularly long crossing.

I'm scared of heights. I have tried to overcome my fear in a million ways—I've even gone bungee jumping once and skydiving twice—but although they were exciting challenges to work through, nothing I've tried has done much to alleviate my fear, and I still try to avoid things like driving across the Golden Gate Bridge unless I absolutely have to. (I did once walk about a third of the way across. I was petrified every step of the way, so I eventually turned around and went back, my heart racing with relief when I finally got back to land.)

I thought for sure I'd be terrified to cross this bridge. I imagined forming a human chain with everyone holding a hand so that I could make it across without becoming paralyzed with terror.

"I know, Rob," Chris said. "There are many bridges along the way. We have no choice but to cross them to continue on the trail."

"Bridge is good," Kumar assured me. "No worries."

Though his reassurance didn't do much to alleviate my anxieties, I realized I just needed to face my fears. So when we came to the foot of the bridge, I took a deep breath, said a prayer, and moved forward.

My legs shook and I kept my hands on the cyclone fencing most of the way, as if that would somehow protect me. What really was protecting me, I figured, were the hundreds of prayer flags tied to the fencing that were fluttering in the wind and, no doubt, taking my prayers for a safe crossing straight to heaven.

Fortunately, the prayers worked, because I not only made it across the bridge but also had no problems with any of the bridges after that.

We would cross about five bridges just that first day and many more up ahead, so I was more than relieved to discover I had one less fear to conquer along the way.

▲▲   ▲▲   ▲▲

After we had hiked about three hours, traversing only three miles, we approached Phakding. I was struck by the number of large, two-story buildings, their blue and red roofs brightening the dark greens of the mountainside village.

As we drew closer, I saw just how colorful many of the buildings were: yellow ochre buildings were trimmed in deep blue, green, or red, and strings of colorful prayer flags were draped everywhere like garlands. Big monuments or memorials of some sort, built of stone and carved with Nepali writing, added a calming, sacred element, and I wondered about how, logistically, a village could be built so high in the mountains. Everything used for construction would have had to be hauled from Lukla.

It would only be later, when we reached far more distant villages at higher elevations, that I would realize just how much work went into basic housing construction. There were no roads for trucking anything in; everything had to be hauled on the backs of men or mules or the more common yak.

There were a number of teahouses in Phakding where hikers could have tea and a meal, and even sleep. We stopped for lunch at a place called the Sunrise Lodge and Restaurant. At first they tried to serve me tea, which everyone drank, but I had to decline. I had stopped consuming caffeine over a decade earlier because of my congenital rhythm issues, and I wasn't going to risk stimulating my heart at that elevation. It was hard communicating that I didn't want their tea without offending them, but in the end they brought me hot mango juice, which was sweet and tasty and soon became my go-to drink during tea breaks.

We ate a meal of yak stew, my first real Nepali meal of the trip. We'd had some curries in Kathmandu, but this was the real deal. It was very tender and tasted a lot like beef—which wasn't at all surprising, since domesticated yak are crossed with cattle and are similar bovines. The stew was tasty, not at all spicy, and was served with lots of potatoes and a tasty flatbread. We would need the protein and carbohydrates, so I ate every last bit of it.

"Yak is good," Kumar said. "You eat yak here. Higher up, the yak is no good. Not fresh. Maybe been up there many months."

I decided to take his advice. I didn't want to be eating any bad food, and since transport was clearly an issue there was no telling how often meat was delivered to the higher altitudes, or even what kind of refrigeration they would have—though perhaps it would not be needed, since it was so cold up there.

After I'd eaten, I realized just how tired I was, and a part of me wanted to just book a room in a teahouse and not go on, but I knew we had to.

"I know, I'm beat, too," Chris said. "To tell you the truth, I don't feel so good. My stomach is kind of queasy."

"That's probably the altitude," I said. "Your body will adjust."

"Yeah, I know, but I sure wish it would adjust sooner."

"I'm tired too," Kendra chimed in. "But it's not a big deal."

"All right," I said and looked at Chris. "You'll be okay?"

"Yeah," she said, "let's do it."

Kumar paid for our meals, and after doing some moderate stretching outside, we hit the trail again.

⛰ ⛰ ⛰

We continued downhill for a way, but eventually the trail began to climb uphill and our legs got a really good workout as we hiked along the roaring and winding Duhd Kosi river. As the trail wound back and forth, zigzagging ever higher, we crossed more swaying bridges and I grew more and more comfortable with each step. We passed bright green, terraced rice fields that had been carved like massive steps into the sides of the hills, and villages not much bigger than a cluster of tiny, ancient homes built of homemade bricks.

Whenever yaks and donkeys carrying heavy loads passed by, we dutifully stepped off the trail, sometimes backing right up against the mountain. Men also passed by carrying even bigger loads, sometimes stacked so big you couldn't even tell there was a human beneath them.

The trails wound around the mountainsides like thin ribbons of dirt. When we reached the turns alongside the edge of the mountain, my fear of heights would kick in as I gingerly made my way along them, hoping I wouldn't run into any aggressive yaks. Other times, the trail was indiscernible as we crossed broad, flat, rocky stretches of land high above the earth. Kumar, with his experience and knowledge of the area, led the way.

Occasionally, we'd see an eagle or a vulture fly overhead, which helped give some sense of our altitude. Vultures can fly quite high, but eagles don't fly much higher than ten thousand feet, so I figured we hadn't gone up too high yet.

I was right. Our destination for the day would be Monjo, a small village about 9,300 feet up, where we would sleep for the night.

▲▲　▲▲　▲▲

By the time we got to Monjo, we'd been hiking for at least five hours. Chris, Kendra, and I, still jet-lagged, were utterly exhausted. We found our room in a teahouse at a place called the Summit Home. It was a fairly large building, made of coursed stone from the area.

"Wow, this place is great," Kendra said as we went inside. "When I hiked Kilimanjaro, we had to sleep in tents."

"I don't think I'd want to sleep in a tent tonight," I said. I was so tired, and every bit of me ached.

The room Kendra and I shared contained only two small beds and a large window overlooking the gorgeous mountains. There was a clean bathroom, with hot water for the shower. We set down our things and went to the community room for tea and hot mango juice.

There were a lot of other hikers in the community room, which sort of surprised me; we'd seen only a smattering along the way. It was nice to sit and chat and hear their different stories. They came from the United States, Canada, and all over Europe. Almost all were young and strong and in good shape.

I felt like I was in terrible shape. Prior to the trip, my training workouts had been mostly every other day, to give my body a rest, but the hiking on the trip was every day. Already, I was completely and totally exhausted. Even my bones felt like they were made of rubber. I went outside and did some stretching to properly cool down my muscles and prevent them from cramping the next day.

After a delicious dinner of *momo*, which is sort of like dim sum dumplings filled with goat meat and spices, we all called it an early night.

As I crawled into my sleeping bag, which wrapped me up from head to toe like a mummy, with nothing but my face exposed to the crisp air, I caught a glance of the two sandwich bags on the windowsill that contained all my medicine bottles. There were vitamins, heart rhythm drugs, and several over-the-counters. There were pills to help lower my cholesterol, reduce my muscle aches, boost my mood, and settle my stomach. In total, I had to take thirteen capsules a day to keep my ill body functioning as normally as possible. Would they be enough to keep me healthy and my body performing okay during the intense days ahead? I sure hoped so.

CHAPTER 19:

MUCH-NEEDED REST

It's a very slow process—two steps forward, one step back—
but I'm inching in the right direction.

—Rob Reiner

The next morning, we were up by seven. Every inch of me hurt; even my skin was sore from the blazing sun. Half our things were strewn about the room from the night before, and we quickly rolled up our sleeping bags and repacked our duffel bags so they'd be ready for the porter when he arrived.

After a light breakfast of a tasty, warm, caffeine-free lemon tea and some fruit, I went outside and did some stretching exercises. It was a chilly but beautiful day. Since I would warm up once we got moving, I had dressed in pants, a light shirt, a hat, and sunglasses, but this time I also added some much-needed sunblock.

Even as sore as we were, Kendra and I were both ready to hit the trail. Chris, however, was in noticeable discomfort and moving like a tortoise.

"I feel like I slept in a cardboard box," she said. "I'm not sure I'm going to make it, I feel so crappy."

"You've done it before, so you can do it again. You'll feel better once you get going," I said, trying to pump her up.

"It's a short hike today," Kumar added, "only four hours."

"Yeah, I know this stretch," Chris grumbled. "It's a real bitch."

"Is it really?" I asked her.

"Yeah, it's straight up."

"It is hard, yes, but after that, it is easier. You will see. Today is hardest part, but very short," Kumar said, smiling at Chris as he tried coaxing her to get moving.

"Well, I'm up for it," Kendra said, as ready to get going as I was.

"All right, let's go," Chris said, even though it was obvious she'd rather just go back to bed.

Chris, Kendra, and I all grunted and groaned as we hoisted our packs onto our backs and set out on the hike. We were heading to Namche Bazaar, only about two miles in distance, but just as Chris had said, the hike was indeed a steep climb that was entirely uphill. Sometimes, there were long staircases that left me panting by the time I reached the top; other times, I wished we'd just brought ladders along, it was so steep.

Every step hurt, but we kept going.

Other than a brief moment when I'd felt an extra, abnormal heartbeat the day before and the expected aches and pains of hiking, I felt great. However, I can't say I wasn't nervous. I was regularly checking my pulse, and though I tried not to show any concerns in front of the others, I kept thinking, *Okay, we've got another eight days. Will I be able to do it?* Stopping was never an option, but I was worried about how hard it would be and how much it would hurt.

Despite how long and arduous the trek was, especially since I was still aching so much from the day before, I was fascinated every step of the way. We passed luscious and beautiful green trees, saw boatloads of donkeys coming out of Monjo, and had breathtaking views of the mountains off in the distance.

"Is that it?" I asked, pointing to a high peak. "Is that Mount Everest?"

"No, Rob, sir," Kumar said, laughing at the question I asked every time we turned a corner and saw a new mountain peak or a familiar one from a different angle. "Be patient."

I had imagined that we would show up and there it would be, all by itself, this big, majestic mountain apart from all the others. Instead, with eight of the world's fourteen tallest peaks in the Himalayas, we were surrounded by mountains everywhere we looked—and none of those in view was Mount Everest. Our perspective was completely distorted. It was like being in the heart of Chicago and trying to spot the Sears Tower (now called Willis Tower) but not being able to see it because all the other buildings were in the way.

Reaching Everest felt like an elusive dream. I'd come so far, but still felt so far away from the goal I was pursuing. It was a dream I wasn't giving up on, however; all I had to do was believe what I knew to be true—we were going to reach it, just as long as we kept putting one foot in front of the other.

As we continued, the footfalls became slower and slower, and Chris began to lag behind, huffing and puffing like she'd never exercised a day in her life. Even though she was the oldest in the group—age fifty-four—that just wasn't like her, and I was beginning to wonder what was wrong. We all slowed our pace so she could keep up.

At this more sluggish pace, we began to talk more. We learned that skinny little Babu was actually twenty-four, older than he looked, and was married and had a child. Kumar, unsurprisingly, was single and dating and seemed to like that status just fine.

As we chatted, I peppered Kumar with questions about the local culture. He told me about the food and the religious symbols, about the four castes (social classes) that distinguish Nepali social status, and about the rules for who can and can't marry whom. Though the separation within the caste arrangement is not as rigid as it once was, he told me, it still exists today.

We also spoke about the impact of the tourist industry in the mountains, which has been a mixed blessing in Nepal. On the one hand, it brings an enormous benefit in terms of jobs and income. Almost all the men are involved in some way with the tourist industry, either as guides, porters, or entrepreneurs. The women work in the tourist industry as well; they are rarely guides and never porters (though I don't doubt that every one of them has twice the strength of an American man!), but they run the farms and small businesses and care for the yaks and children.

Nepali women also cook the meals, which requires far more time and effort than we're accustomed to since they can't just run to the grocery store and stock up. Almost everything they eat they grow or raise themselves. After harvesting and storing the food, they cook over open fires, hauling in the wood from the nearest tree stand. And once they get the wood home, it can take hours to prepare a family meal.

Washing the dishes after a meal is another challenging task if you don't have fresh water. Since most villages in the Himalayas don't have a piping system connected to the extensive assortment of rivers, rain, or melted snow in the area and much of the accessible water is polluted, more than a quarter of the population does not have fresh drinking water, and the women spend much of their time scavenging for this basic resource with containers and jugs.

As tourism has brought in more money, some people have switched to gas for cooking, but they still must haul the jugs of petrol home, which isn't exactly like driving the car to the grocery store.

On the other hand, the tourism industry also has brought a life of servitude to the Sherpas, who were once subsistence farmers, as well as a tremendous sense of inequality as they witness *mikaru* (their term for foreigners) coming from all over the world and paying more than some Sherpas make in a lifetime just for the opportunity to climb a mountain. Yet as much as the tourism industry also has created a sense of inequality, it has also created opportunity within the Sherpa culture: a skilled guide can make up to eight times the average annual income of a Nepali.

With tourists come trash—and land erosion, too, as thousands hike the trails every year.

In addition to setting up tourists' camps, serving as their guides on hikes, and carrying their gear, it's the Sherpas who install the fixed ropes and rebuild the trails.

Perhaps the biggest impact of tourism, though, has been the loss of Nepali life. When a *mikaru* dies on the mountain, it makes the news. However, when a Sherpa dies trying to help or save them, it's rarely noted. Since 1950, about 250 Sherpas have died helping tourists on Mount Everest, and each year adds several more. A lot of people assume that because they're more biologically adapted to the higher altitudes, Sherpas aren't affected by altitude sickness, but that's not true. Many do die from it, and with hardly any warning.

Also, far too many die from accidents, falls, or natural disasters. The year prior to my trip, in the disastrous avalanche of April 18, 2014, sixteen Sherpas were buried alive. They had been trying to fix ropes, lay trails, and haul oxygen, tents, and stoves for a *mikaru* expedition. Another eight had died the year before that, and since the men who scale the mountains are young or middle-aged, almost all leave behind families.

As we hiked with Kumar and Babu, I couldn't help but reflect on the steep price the Sherpas pay for our adventures. Of course, most of those deaths were at the higher elevations, beyond Base Camp, but as we hiked and passed many *chorten*, Buddhist memorials for climbers who had died in the mountains, I was humbled to realize the danger we faced and the even greater danger guides like Kumar and Babu faced every day.

Despite this, I still felt we would somehow be safe, that those catastrophes happened to other people. After all, I had survived near-death experiences enough times that I was confident I'd be spared yet again.

As we continued chatting and learning about the Sherpas, we entered Sagarmatha National Park, Nepal's first national park to be recognized as a World Heritage Site by the United Nations in 1979. Sagarmatha—which translates as "Forehead of the Sea or Sky" and "Mother of the Universe"—is also the highest national park in the world, reaching more than 29,000 feet above sea level at the top of Mount Everest. I was overwhelmed by the scenery as we hiked through the area, climbing more stone stairs and crossing long, swaying bridges that just the day before had terrified me.

At one point, we reached a spot with two suspension bridges that crossed over the gorgeous Dudh Kosi Gorge. The newer and higher passage, made up of prayer flags and metal wire, was named the Hillary Bridge. The lower, unused span was the Larja Bridge. There was something about it—the beautiful view of the river valley coupled with the tree-covered mountains—that took my breath away. As I paused to take in the sounds of the roaring river, the call of birds flying overhead, and the jingle of bells on passing donkeys, I realized we were indeed far from the world we'd come from.

Beneath our feet was solid rock, and each footfall was a reminder that if we slipped or fell, severe injury, possibly even death, awaited us.

Yes, today was really difficult, but as we drew closer to Namche Bazaar, I began to think that if this was the toughest stretch, it wouldn't be such a hard hike to make after all. I was tough enough for whatever was up ahead.

It was a false confidence, I would soon discover.

▲▲ ▲▲ ▲▲

After a few hours, we reached Namche Bazaar, a village of more than 1,500 people that stands at an elevation of 11,000 feet. When Edmund Hillary and Tenzing Norgay first reached the summit of Mount Everest in 1953, the village was nothing more than a scattering of huts. Now, as the last point up the mountain where hikers can stock up on goods and warm clothes, it is practically a thriving metropolis.

We were staying at the Namche Hotel, a simple, four-story building in the midst of this colorful village.

"I just want to lie down," Chris said as she dropped her bag to the ground and sat down to rest. "I feel like crap and my head hurts. How are you doing, Rob?"

"I'm good, just exhausted."

As for Kendra, she was pretty fit and seemed to be handling herself quite well, though she, too, was exhausted and aching.

We had another nice room that night—the nicest we would stay in during the trek. The quality accommodations, warm beds, and showers that awaited us were a welcome surprise. Although the rooms still had no heat, they were spacious and had large windows that brought in lots of light. It was pleasant during the day with the sunlight and temperatures, but we had to conserve heat in our mummy bags when we went to bed. Each night, we would fill up our water bottles with boiling hot water and place them by our feet to stay warm when we went to bed. The next day, the water would be cool, and we would use it as drinking water during our hike.

By this point, we'd ascended to cloud-cover level, and the clouds had obscured the mountains. Outside, an eerie, romantic mist floated on the air, with trees poking their way through the curdling grey, and I felt, for the first time, that we were truly in the mountains, higher than the eagles fly.

It was early afternoon, so we all took a nap—what became a daily routine on our trip—then had some tea and hot mango juice, after which we walked around town. There were many teahouses and shops selling memorabilia and knockoff name-brand clothing and equipment. Chris had gotten a massage from The Real Professional Massage Therapy on her previous hike, and she'd been talking about getting another one there since we began our hike. The three of us walked to the shop and, given our tired muscles, all made appointments. Chris went for hers right away, Kendra would go for hers after that. I scheduled my own for the following day.

With the free time I had, I decided to head back to the hotel and try to catch up on email and blog posts on my laptop, which I'd been carrying on my back throughout the hike. Although we did have internet at points in the mountains, it was painfully slow. I had no idea that this evening would be the last one on our trek on which I'd have the energy to write.

▲▲ ▲▲ ▲▲

"Oh my god," Chris said after returning from her massage. "My legs hurt so bad. I feel much better. If only they could do the same for my head."

With praise like that, I couldn't wait for my own massage the next day to help with my aches—especially since back home, I get massaged almost every week to help with my muscular dystrophy.

After Kendra returned from her appointment, we met for dinner and spent a long time speaking with Ang May Sherpa, the woman who ran the hotel and teahouse. Her husband, Ang Dorjee Sherpa, was chairman of the Sagarmatha Pollution Control Committee (SPCC), a community of ice doctors that checks the conditions of the ice every season and sets the ladders and fixes the ropes along the icefall route for climbers looking to summit Mount Everest. Their work is extremely important; many lives depend on it.

After a good dinner of more yak and *momo*, we went to our rooms to get ready for bed. I monitored my heart, and it was still going strong. The next day, an acclimation day, we would be hiking up to Everest View Hotel and trying to get our first glimpse of Mount Everest before coming back to Namche.

It was another beautiful day and hike. We went for a few hours before reaching a large, two-story building in the middle of nowhere. There was a big staircase leading up to the entrance, and the moment I saw it I burst ahead of everyone and ran up the stairs like Sylvester Stallone in *Rocky*, victoriously raising my fists and hiking poles in the air when I reached the top.

Then I bent over and panted like an old man, I was so worn out from the grueling hike. Still, it was well worth every gasp of cold air, I felt so inspired.

While enjoying some afternoon tea and mango juice, we sat outside with a gorgeous view of the mountains. Unfortunately, though, there were some clouds in the air that shielded Mount Everest from view. I would just have to wait a little bit longer.

The hike down from Everest View Hotel was steep and difficult on our legs, and I couldn't wait for my massage when we got back in the afternoon. It turned out to be nothing like I was used to—the pressure was lighter than the deep-tissue sports massages I typically got—but the masseuse focused mostly on my legs, which was exactly what I needed. It helped soothe the soreness in my muscles and increase my circulation, and, yes, my legs felt so much better afterwards.

At dinner, we talked about having a second acclimation day in Namche. We were scheduled to hike to Thame—what we learned was a beautiful little town where Sherpas live—but it was a full day's hike, and in the opposite direction of where we would be heading for Base Camp. Since Chris still wasn't feeling well and Kendra and I weren't keen on going an entire day out of the way to see a small village in the middle of nowhere, we decided to bag that idea and relax in Namche instead.

Staying in Namche proved to be the right decision: when we woke up the next morning, there was snow everywhere. It was wild to go from the beautiful sunshine that had filled the past several days to feeling like we were in a Chicago snowstorm. It looked super cold. Plus, despite the massage I'd gotten the day before, every bone in my body ached.

Hanging out in Namche and exploring the little town turned out to be a great day and exactly what we needed. By the next morning, Chris, who was feeling a little better, was ready to give trekking another try. After a light breakfast and some indoor stretching to prepare for the day's journey, we hit the muddy trail, ready to push our weary bodies to new heights.

CHAPTER 20:

HIGHER AND HIGHER

A man's reach should exceed his grasp or what's heaven for?
—Robert Browning

O ur next stop was Khumjung, 13,024 feet above sea level. Despite the higher elevation, the hike wasn't nearly as steep as the hike from Monjo to Namche, but it was far longer. Trying to avoid the lethargy I'd felt after eating the first day, I didn't want to break for lunch.

"Robby, I don't think I can make it without taking more breaks," Chris said. She was still moving at a snail's pace, and I was starting to think something might actually be wrong. She normally wasn't like that. My hope was that she was simply out of shape, and I convinced myself that the more she hiked, the easier it would get.

Normally, when Chris and I traveled together, our typical pattern was to be mad at each other by day three. Whether it was having Kendra as a buffer, the magnitude of the trip, or the time Chris and I had spent repairing our relationship, I found myself with a great deal of patience and caring on this journey, which pretty much eliminated the usual tension. Unfortunately, Chris wasn't enjoying the hike at all, I could tell, and as the day progressed, I realized my sister was in trouble. I tried my best to encourage her every time she muttered that she wasn't going to make it, but deep down I began to wonder myself.

We reached Khumjung by late afternoon. The path leading up to the cluster of blue-and green-roofed buildings was lined on either side by a stone wall about three feet high, giving the village the feel of a tiny kingdom. We all spun the prayer wheels when we arrived; then we stopped to get our rooms at the Ama Dablam View Lodge before grabbing a quick lunch.

After lunch, we took a half-hour hike to Kunde Hospital, a small clinic originally founded in 1966 by Sir Edmund Hillary and wholly staffed by Nepalese doctors and health workers. It was a very simple hospital, and we passed many cute children playing outside along the way. After knocking on some doors, we were greeted by a friendly doctor. When we introduced ourselves and explained about my health problems and the purpose of our trek, he was more than happy to speak with us and show us around.

After spending almost an hour visiting the hospital and speaking with the doctor, we walked back to Khumjung and checked out the school Hillary had built for the local children. With humble beginnings of only two classrooms, Khumjung School now provides education for more than 350 students in preschool through high school. For some reason, it was closed. However, we took the opportunity to walk around and I played like a child on some monkey bars before we returned to the lodge.

▲▲ ▲▲ ▲▲

By the following morning, most of the snow had melted and it looked like it would be a good, albeit slippery, day to hike.

It was time to hit the trail for Deboche—Yeti country. Yeti are abominable snowmen who, legend has it, roam throughout the Himalayas, and we were approaching the region where there have allegedly been many sightings. Even Sir Edmund Hillary reported seeing giant footprints near the summit—though he did discount the Yeti legend, choosing instead to believe they were the footprints of some other creature.

As for me, I just got a kick out of the idea that abominable snowmen might be watching us as we hiked—and though they may have seen us, we didn't see them. What we did see were lots of yaks and Sherpas, occasional hikers, and colorful Nepali artwork painted onto the rocks.

It was a steep hike, and one of our longest. We passed through some amazing scenery and planned a lunch break and visit in the village of Tengboche, home to the largest monastery in the region.

Unfortunately, Chris was really struggling again. She hadn't been getting better with the hike; she'd been getting worse each day. Still, I encouraged her, hoping all she needed was a push. With her experience, I was convinced she'd be able to make it—and knowing she was a nurse and Kumar was an experienced guide, I felt confident she was in good hands. The best I could do, I decided, was to continue to support her.

I fell into step with her midway through the day's hike. "You're looking good, sis," I said. "How are you feeling?"

"Okay, Robby," she replied. "I can make it. I don't want you going up there without me."

I knew Chris was worried about me as much as I was worried about her.

"Cool," I said, "because I don't want to get there without you." A part of me, however, felt bad that maybe I had created too much pressure for her to be with me, as she knew how badly I wanted a big hug from her in celebration of what we'd accomplished once we reached Base Camp.

After a brief rest, which was becoming more frequent by the day, we continued up and down the sloping trail. It was an amazing hike. We passed through a rhododendron forest with beautiful pink flowers in full bloom. We saw lots of mountain goats along the trail, and far more Sherpas than we'd seen up to that point, carrying equipment from town to town. The loads on their backs were enormous, and I couldn't help but marvel at their seemingly superhuman strength.

It had been a beautiful day, but in the late morning, it began to turn bitter cold. Just as we reached Tengboche, it began to snow.

We stopped for lunch at Café Tengboche, which houses the famous Tengboche Bakery, one of the highest-altitude bakeries in the world.

Since the lower air pressure at the higher elevation causes the sugar to be more concentrated and the baked goods to rise faster, adjustments have to be made for baking temperatures and times. Alas, I did not see if these baked goods tasted any differently; we warmed up with soup, tea, and hot mango juice, and didn't partake in the pastries.

After lunch, we were able to leave our equipment in the café and walk to the monastery, only about a hundred yards away. It felt great walking without our poles and packs on our backs.

Much like the entrance for Tengboche, an archway led into the monastery—a pink one that was flanked by colorful, mythical Buddhist lions on each side. After walking up four separate sets of stairs, with the last having more than twenty-five steps, I realized that we had to remove our shoes before entering. After hiking all day, my back was aching and my feet were throbbing and cold. The last thing I wanted to do was bend over and take off my shoes.

"Come on, Rob," Chris said, "you're not going inside unless you do."

Kendra wordlessly took off her shoes as I struggled to take mine off too.

Inside, we were warmly greeted by some monks. In the distance, another monk read aloud. I watched him, mesmerized by his concentration and calm. Then I quietly purchased a candle and approached the Buddhist altar, where I lit the candle and murmured a prayer for our safe ascent and for Chris to get better.

The monastery was so peaceful that I immediately felt grounded, and a gentle wave of serenity washed over me. I breathed deeply and thought about why I was there and what I was doing. The whole meaning of the trip was to defy my body's decline, to prove to myself that my life was not coming to an end but simply transforming, and I would continue to reach even greater heights. As much as my body ached, I knew I was achieving exactly what I set out to do. I was hiking to the world's highest mountain, and my heart couldn't be stronger or happier. If only my head could shake the foreboding sense that everything was about to change.

We still had a ways to go before reaching Deboche, and the weather had turned miserable. It was cold and raining, and the trail had become slippery mud. We all had to use our poles for balance to avoid falling down the mountain into the raging river below. We crossed several more bridges along the way, and the wetness and strong winds made them feel more threatening. The peaceful sense that had filled me in the monastery had washed away. Now I was grumpy and uncomfortable and just wanted to get to Deboche.

We hadn't yet passed the tree line, but we knew we were getting closer to Base Camp, even though we still had a few more days of hiking left. In the meantime, an amazing view of Mount Ama Dablam served as a reminder that Mount Everest was just around the bend. With every step, I grew more excited.

When we finally reached the village of Deboche, over 12,500 feet high, we were exhausted, somber, and freezing. As had been the case in each of the hotels we'd stayed at so far, there was no heat in the rooms. I quickly put my things away and headed to the lodge's restaurant, where people were gathered around a stove in the middle of the room, trying to stay warm. I sat there for hours, chatting and swapping tales with other hikers, each of us doing our best to keep warm in the bone-chilling cold of the mountain air.

▲▲ ▲▲ ▲▲

The next morning, we were up and at it again, heading to Dingboche, a hike that would take us a full six to seven hours. Chris continued to groan in pain but she carried on. Kendra spent the hike speaking with Babu, with his rudimentary English, as they hurried ahead of us. I continued to struggle with the cold and the climb. I never had worked so strenuously for so long as I had in the last several days. It was as exhausting as it was exciting, but we were so close to our final goal.

Soon we passed the tree line, and the trail transformed into an eerie, lunar landscape of rock and shrub. We had an amazing view of Mount Ama Dablam, a jagged, bluish-white peak that looked almost as if it were blocking our way, it was so close and large. There was little native wildlife at this altitude—at least, little that I noticed—but there were some birds flying overhead and scurrying around the rocks, somehow surviving the increasingly thinning air we were struggling to breathe. The hike had become exponentially more difficult due to the higher altitude, and each step of the way was as much an effort as a victory.

We hadn't gone far when we came to a bridge that had completely collapsed. Had anyone been on it when it did, they would have plummeted to their deaths. Fortunately, Kumar told us, it had collapsed in the off-season, so no one was hurt. Unfortunately, seeing it did nothing for my confidence and fear of heights.

We ended up hiking farther downhill to a much smaller bridge and hiked back up again after crossing, making our long day's hike even longer. The landscape was beautiful, however, which helped.

We saw more farming lots and huts along the way. Many had yak dung plastered along the outside walls so it would dry out in the sun. Yaks are a highly respected animal in the region and are often individually named, like children. They are said to give off little odor, and their bodies, hair, and excrement have multiple uses, including a clean and inexpensive resource for fuel.

After what seemed like an eternity of struggling to hike and to breathe—as well as a stop for tea in a small village called Shomare—we made it to Dingboche, just as it was beginning to snow. We got rooms at the Hotel Good Luck, where we stayed through the evening as well as the next day for what would be our second and final acclimation stop of the climb.

On our acclimation day, we hiked to Nangkartshang Hill. Each day had included some spectacular views, but the hill was something extraordinary. It was a two-hour hike from our hotel—more than 1,500 feet above the village of Dingboche—and the scenery was absolutely gorgeous. It included the mountains of Kangtega, Ama Dablam, Nuptse, Lhotse, and Makalu. Once atop the hill, we posed for several pictures with the glorious background and sat and talked for more than an hour. It was the first day we'd really stopped to appreciate the beauty we were engulfed in.

The next morning, we were headed for Lobuche at 16,109 feet, a nearly five-hour trek from Dingboche. Kumar and I hiked slowly to keep pace with Chris while Kendra and Babu hurried ahead. On the way to Lobuche we would walk through Thokla Pass, a memorial site that would add a somber tone to the hike. There we would see many stone memorials, or *chotun*, erected in memory of climbers who had died, including one for Scott Fisher, an expedition leader who died in the tragic 1996 expedition that killed eight climbers when a blizzard struck. That was the expedition Jon Krakauer wrote about for his book *Into Thin Air* and has been the subject of a couple of IMAX movies, most recently *Everest*.

I spun the spool-like prayer wheels that ran along the length of one stretch of the path and prayed for a safe hike for us all, for my heart to hold out, and for Chris to feel better.

After a couple hours, we were only a few steps away from the entrance of Thokla Pass when we saw a horse carrying an enormous load slip and fall on the rocky incline ahead of us. The Sherpa who was accompanying it showed no pity, angrily striking the horse again and again, trying to beat it into resuming its arduous hike. As we watched, it became clear that it was an old horse that could not raise itself back up and continue up the trail, especially with so much weight on its back. I desperately wanted to help and asked Kumar if I could lend a hand, but he suggested I stay away, that my offer would be very unwelcome.

We stood back and observed, each of us horrified by the sight but helpless to assist. Eventually, some other Sherpas came along and aided the man, and they finally started unloading some of the weight from the horse. When all the equipment had been removed from its back the horse struggled back onto its feet, but the Sherpas paid it no mind. All their focus was on the equipment spread across the trail; they couldn't have cared less about the animal that was suffering so badly.

By this point, we had hiked around the horse and were watching from a higher elevation, but I couldn't take it anymore. I walked back down, took the horse's reins, and walked it up the steep passage.

When we were finally up on level ground, the Sherpa who had been beating the horse returned and began to reload all the heavy equipment onto the poor beast's back. Whether it survived the journey, I'll never know, but a part of me prayed that it hadn't, that it instead had been released to the heavens, where it would no longer serve as a beast of burden.

I turned my attention back to our team and was awestruck. We were standing in the middle of what looked like a cemetery full of tombstones. There were hundreds of rock memorials surrounding us, and there were prayer flags strung from one end of the hill to other.

"Look, Rob!" Chris said. "There is the memorial for Scott Fisher."

I simply nodded my head, speechless, as I looked around in amazement.

It was a special moment, to be surrounded by these memorials— a lovely recognition of these inspiring people's attempts to maneuver through unpredictable mountains. Now, here we were, following in their footsteps, not letting the risks deter us from our goal.

⛰ ⛰ ⛰

At last, we made it to Lobuche and checked in at the Himalayan Eco Resort. We were surprised to see the Chilean team there as well, and it was fun to catch up with them. I couldn't imagine what was in store for them. They would be continuing on beyond Base Camp to the summit of Mount Everest, then back down, and then hiking to the summit of Lhotse. It seemed impossible to me, given how exhausted and sore we all were. However, it also sounded exhilarating, and as much as I looked forward to a warm bed in the near future, a part of me envied them on their adventure.

After another hot meal of soup and potatoes and an early night, we were back at it by sunrise and making our way to Gorak Shep, where we would have our last night before reaching Base Camp. Before we left, the Chilean videographer Fernando, impressed with my story, asked if he could do an interview of me for the documentary he was filming of Ernesto and Rodrigo's amazing expedition.

I couldn't believe it was finally happening—we were nearing the base of Mount Everest, the 17,500-foot goal my doctors had told me I could never reach. I would be reaching it within forty-eight hours—yet I feared my sister might not.

Chris had truly fallen ill by this point; it was clear she was suffering from altitude sickness and was in real pain. We were so close—so very close—but by the time we reached Gorak Shep, which is just under

17,000 feet and rests on a frozen, sand-covered lakebed, it was clear my continued prayers throughout the trip hadn't been answered. I was utterly thrilled to have reached the village; Base Camp was practically next door. Chris, however, looked terrible. She was grimacing and pale. For the first time, I realized she could be in grave danger.

"I can make it," she said. "It's not much farther."

"You sure?" I asked.

"Yeah," she said, "I've done it before. I'll make it."

The Chilean team had arrived before us, and when Ernesto saw how sick Chris was, he rummaged around in his pack and pulled out a pulse oximeter, which measures the oxygen level in blood and determines how much good oxygen is moving from our hearts to our extremities. Normal levels are in the nineties. All of us tested in the eighties, which is typical for such a high altitude—except for Chris, who tested in the fifties.

"That's not good," Ernesto said.

"No, it's not," Chris agreed. As a climber, she wanted to keep going. As a nurse, she knew she was in trouble. "Let me call Jiban and see what he thinks. Then I'll take a nap and meet you all for dinner."

That seemed like a good plan. Chris went up to her room and called Jiban while I went up to my room to take a nap.

A short while later, she knocked at my door.

"What'd he say?" I asked, assuming he'd simply told her to take it easy.

"He said he's sending a helicopter to get me out," she answered. "I have to pack and be at the helipad in fifteen minutes."

I was so worried for her. She had struggled throughout the entire trip, pushing forward to join me at Base Camp, and now here she was, plagued with a serious medical condition that could turn fatal. We both knew Jiban was right: she had to descend.

Suddenly, everything had shifted. One minute we were getting ready for a nap, the next we were rushing to get Chris evacuated.

"What's going on?" Kendra asked. "Is everything okay?"

I explained the situation. "We have to get Chris to the helipad right away," I told her.

"Oh my god," she said. "I'll go with you."

▲▲ ▲▲ ▲▲

The helipad, essentially an area of flat rocks at the top of a hill, was not much more than a hundred yards away from the hotel, but it was a very steep climb, and damn chilly. Kumar and Babu led the way as I helped carry Chris's things. When we got to the helipad, the helicopter wasn't there yet, but we soon saw it approaching, and we all hugged Chris good-bye as it drew close. Though it was a difficult time, the helicopter descending from the sky and landing on the flat rock formation being used as a helipad was an amazing sight.

With the help of the others, Chris climbed in. As the chopper rose from the earth, it whipped the freezing cold air into a stinging windstorm. It was really loud for a minute, with things flying all over the place, but in an instant the helicopter was gone and the area became completely quiet and desolate again.

We walked back to our rooms in silence.

▲▲ ▲▲ ▲▲

Later that evening, I talked to Chris on the phone; she had made it safely back to Lukla and would fly back to Kathmandu the following morning.

As for the rest of our group still in the mountains, we had to make a decision about what to do the following day. We could spend another day acclimatizing in Gorak Shep with a hike up to Kala Patthar, a notable landmark off the route, or we could proceed straight to Everest Base Camp, where we would spend the night.

With an elevation of more than 18,500 feet, Kala Patthar is almost a thousand feet higher than Everest Base Camp and provides the best view of Mount Everest. Several trekkers along the way had mentioned the sunrise there was absolutely incredible, and Kumar agreed. We'd never have another chance to see such an amazing sight, so we decided to do both: wake up at 3:00 a.m. the next day and hike up in time to catch the rising sun in Kala Patthar and then later make our way to Base Camp.

We would come to learn in about a week's time how crucial that decision would prove to be.

CHAPTER 21:

REACHING THE SUMMIT

People do not decide to become extraordinary. They decide to accomplish extraordinary things.

—Edmund Hillary

Though the hike from Gorak Shep to Kala Patthar was only one to two hours, it was a huge change in elevation. Due to the combination of the predawn hour and higher altitude, the temperature was freezing cold—and felt even colder with the stiff breeze.

We had dressed in our warmest weather gear; I was wearing thick gloves and an insulated hat that seemed to do little good. After only a short while, my fingers were frozen stiff, and it was hard to hold on to my hiking poles as I climbed the steep, icy trail. I could see there were already maybe fifteen to twenty people on the trail.

If they can do it, then so can I.

It was incomprehensibly cold. I couldn't feel my hands and could barely feel my face. It was difficult to breathe and even more difficult to talk. Every step was a struggle, and we reached a point where I needed a break every fifteen to twenty steps.

After what had happened to Chris, Kumar was watching me closely.

"You are getting sick," he said. "Altitude sickness. You need to stop."

I wasn't going to stop, not when I was that close.

"I can make it," I mumbled. My face felt completely frozen, as if every syllable I uttered could shatter it.

I had no idea how I'd do it; all I knew was that I was going to do it. I was filled with determination. One way or another, I'd push through the pain and discomfort and continue on. Turning back was not an option.

We were three-quarters of the way up. As always, Kendra and Babu were way ahead of me and Kumar. I wanted to keep going, but Kumar continued to worry.

"It's not safe for you," he said. "Stop here." Then he pointed toward the sky, and I saw it: my first substantial view of Mount Everest, the iconic view I'd seen on postcards and pictures of the majestic mountain towering over the Himalayas, just as the sun began to rise. It was gorgeous, remarkable, indescribable. I was stunned into silence.

Kumar began to rationalize with me, a tactic I had not expected.

"Rob, sir," he said, "the view further up will be no different. It will be the same. Save your strength, save your strength for Base Camp!"

I thought about it. Kala Patthar was not why I was here. Kala Patthar was supposed to be an acclimation day, and I had already climbed higher than Base Camp—we were at almost 18,000 feet. I could see the top; it was not far from where we were. I could see the people turning back around. I did not need to go farther.

"All right," I reluctantly said, my face stinging. "We can go back."

As long as I made it to Base Camp, I would reach my goal.

Still, it was the worst day of the trip for me; I felt defeated. After all the training I'd done and after losing Chris the day before, I didn't want to turn back. But my body just wouldn't allow me to go farther, and I needed to listen to it. These thoughts fought back and forth in my head, but in the end, it was the best sunrise I'd ever seen in my life, so for that, it was worth it.

We hadn't eaten before the hike, so as soon as we got back to Gorak Shep we had breakfast. I was back in bed by 9:00 a.m., and when I woke up at lunchtime, I felt great. My body was rested and I was ready for a rematch, for the battle to continue. Base Camp was just another hour and a half away, and I couldn't wait to get there.

Most people don't have the opportunity to stay at Base Camp overnight; they typically trek up to a small dedicatory of rocks with commemorative inscriptions on them, then hike back down and spend the evening again at Gorak Shep. I, however, wanted to know what the experience of sleeping at the base of Mount Everest would be like, so Jiban had arranged to have a tent set up and waiting for us when we got there. I couldn't have been more excited for that freezing-cold night to begin. I was ready and able, and I would not be defeated again.

As we hiked, with Babu and Kendra ahead, Kumar and me trudging behind, I felt emotionally overwhelmed. I was thrilled and excited and proud to be finally reaching Mount Everest. At the same time, I was devastated that Chris was gone, and sick with worry about her. It seemed as if every emotion human beings are capable of feeling was swirling around inside me.

I moved slowly in the afternoon—more slowly than usual given the difficulties I'd experienced that morning. It seemed as if the hour-and-a-half hike was taking twice as long as it should. I felt my anger rise throughout the day, frustrated that Kendra and Babu were so far ahead, not waiting for me to catch up. It hadn't been as much of an issue when Chris was with me to keep me company. Kumar was friendly and great, but still, I missed my sister.

I pushed my anger aside and focused on my goal. And finally, there it was—or there it was not. In the midst of the trail was a pile of rocks and stones with prayer flags and signs plastered alongside to meet trekkers as they arrived that read: "Welcome to Base Camp" and "Everest Base Camp 2015."

I'd done it!

Wait, I thought, *is this really it?*

I wasn't prepared for how big it was, and it felt like we were in the middle of nowhere.

Kendra and Babu, who already had arrived, greeted us with celebratory hugs and talked excitedly about reaching our goal.

"Check this out," Kendra said. "You did it!"

I didn't feel like I'd done it. Where was the Chilean team? They were supposed to be there. It was as if we'd gone to the moon only to find we were lost in space.

Kumar explained. Though we had reached some stone markers welcoming us to Base Camp, we hadn't reached the camp itself. We were isolated on the mountain, more than two miles away from the last of the teahouses at Gorak Shep but still more than a mile away from the tents and mountaineers staged near the base of the Khumbu Icefall, located at the head of the Khumbu Glacier.

Like a child, I couldn't help but ask Kumar, "How much longer?"

"Not far, Rob, sir," he said patiently. "We're almost there."

I thought we'd reach the tents in no time, so I was surprised to find that as long as it felt like we'd been hiking, they didn't seem to be getting any closer. The hike continued for another good hour or so. As we moved up and down the ridges of the glacier, Kumar and I once again found ourselves alone, with Kendra and Babu way ahead. I couldn't keep up; my feet were getting heavier and my breaths deeper with every step.

Up to this point in the trek, I had not fallen, but on this final part of the ascent, I slipped and fell twice. We were on uneven, rocky, icy terrain—but both falls occurred as I was speaking into my camera while shooting a video (clearly not the safest way to navigate the final and most difficult stretch of the trip).

The collection of tents in the distance looked easy enough to reach, but the distance was deceptive, like a mirage in the desert.

We continued along the Khumbu Glacier, which is the world's highest glacier and spans more than six miles. Because this gradually moving river of ice is nestled between Mount Everest and the Lhotse–Nuptse ridge, we found ourselves in a plateau of sorts in the midst of the mountains. Straight in front of us, we could see Khumbutse, then Changtse, the West Shoulder of Mount Everest, Mount Everest itself, Lhotse a little further back, and finally Nuptse. The mountains were spectacular, and the blue of the sky was transparent on this crystal-clear afternoon.

"Where's our tent?" I asked Kumar.

"I don't know," he said, "but it should be over there somewhere." He pointed off to the left, where we could see a group of tents in the distance.

His response didn't help to put me at ease, but I found solace in the fact that the uphill portion of the adventure seemed to be over. I continued to move forward, albeit slowly.

Kumar spoke up. "You wait here, Rob; I'll find the tent."

"Okay, but when you do, don't forget to come get me!" I joked.

"I won't forget you, Rob, sir," he said, smiling.

Kumar took off and I sat down on a rock formation. There, deep in thought, I found peace.

This is AWESOME, I'm actually here! I reminded myself over and over.

Even after all the bad stuff of the day, the horrible hike to Kala Patthar, the loss of my sister, I still made it. I had reached the seemingly unattainable. I had climbed the Himalayas to rest at the base of Mount Everest.

The journey to get here had been grueling on multiple levels.

Mentally, I was exhausted from all the "project manager" duties—coordinating all my doctor's appointments, managing the communication among offices, scheduling my flights, and following up on all my massage, physical training, and hiking trips. It had been a daunting task, and my head had been spinning like a tornado throughout the entire process. It would have been easy to give up when Chris got sick and was forced to end her hike early, but my upbringing didn't teach me to take the easy way out.

Physically, there were so many days during my training that I didn't want to get off the couch or out of bed, or to put my aging body through the fatigue and pain that went along with training, but I knew that living my life to the fullest didn't always equate to taking the painless way out. When I came home feeling like I got run over by a dump truck, I'd soak my aching, deteriorating body in Epsom salt baths and elevate and cover my sore limbs with ice packs.

Perhaps most of all, the trip had been spiritually and emotionally grueling. I'd had to continually tell myself I could do it—that I wanted to do it—and remind myself *why* I was doing it. Although there were five of us going up together, and the mountains were filled with people, I had never felt so completely and utterly isolated, as if I were alone with the universe trying to find some higher purpose, not just in my journey but in my life and in my damaged body.

I worried about my sister, I worried about myself, and I was frustrated with the lack of teamwork and support from physicians and others throughout this process who had questioned my ability. I'd been afraid many times—afraid of falling, of slipping, of having heart issues, and sometimes even of not making it. I had often felt deflated and sad, too—sad that Chris was too sick to enjoy the trip, and sad that upon reaching this pinnacle, I wouldn't have someone special to share it with.

For whom am I struggling? I wondered.

Will I reach people with my journey?

Will I be appreciated?

Will this matter?

Each of those questions elicited the same answer from within: I had no idea. However, when I dug deeper, an alternative response came to mind. As much as I wanted support and to reach and inspire others with my story, this journey was for *me*. My thoughts and prayers were guiding me, and God was my witness.

It was the hardest thing I'd ever done . . . on purpose!

▲▲ ▲▲ ▲▲

Finally, after what felt like about an hour, Kumar returned from scouting out the tent situation.

"Come, Rob, sir," he said. "I found the tent!"

I followed him across the glacier, weaving around dozens of tents along the way. There were different tents for cooking, eating, and sleeping, and even a small one with a bucket inside to use as a toilet. Deep within the maze, there was a large group tent with a banner on the side reading, "Welcome to Chilean Everest & Lhotse Expedition." As we moved closer, we noticed Kendra, Babu, and the Chilean team all gathered inside.

I so badly wanted Chris to be there, to give me the victory hug I had so longed for. Instead, much to my surprise, Ernesto rose from his chair, walked directly to me, and hugged me tightly. Rodrigo and Fernando soon followed, congratulating me on having made it and giving me the greatest man hugs ever. I was filled with joy. All my training couldn't have prepared me for the weakness I felt in that moment; I was overcome with emotion, happier than I ever could have imagined!

There was one more thing I wanted a picture of: one of our whole group with the banner Jiban had made for us at the Yak & Yeti. I'd asked him to send it with the gear and food he had flown up for the Chileans, so I started asking around and finally Kumar found it among the supplies he'd sent for the base camp cook, who prepares all the meals for the expedition teams.

We unraveled the banner and took it up by the small yellow tent that had been set up for me to spend the night in. After I took some pictures with just me and Kumar, the entire team joined us for some shots in front of the Khumbu Icefall—which, because of its deep crevasses, towering ice seracs, and avalanche-prone terrain, is one of the most treacherous places on Mount Everest for climbers.

That day, I met one of the most inspiring women I've ever encountered: Melissa Arnot, then a thirty-two-year-old American emergency medical technician and mountaineer who had reached the summit of Everest five times. Chris had met her on her previous hiking expedition, and I was familiar with her achievements. Melissa was so warm and welcoming, taking the time to speak with me in her tent and introducing me to the rest of her expedition team. She was really supportive when I told her my story but I was even more impressed by her. She was attempting her sixth climb to the summit—this time without the use of oxygen.

For years, the thought of climbing Mount Everest without the use of supplemental oxygen was considered physically impossible due to the lower air pressure and the breathing difficulties it caused. Now it has been proven possible, but even so, of the more than 4,000 people who have reached the top of Earth's highest mountain since Edmund Hillary and Tenzing Norgay first summited in 1953, less than two hundred of them have done it without the use of oxygen.

After chatting with everyone, snapping pictures, and just basking in the incredible feat I'd attained, I was ready to collapse. Unfortunately, it turned out to be an incredibly cold and uncomfortable night. The altitude was so high, I really struggled to breathe. Something as simple as turning over in my sleeping bag would make me out of breath, and it would take several minutes for me to calm down and breathe normally again.

At one point in the night, I woke up needing to go to the bathroom. The tent was only about thirty feet away, but it was a struggle to sit up, to put on my boots, zip up my coat, and walk there.

As I returned to my tent, the darkness lifted only by my headlamp and the moonlight above, I looked up at the gorgeous sky and toward Khumbu Icefall. The scene was majestic. It was like I was staring into infinity, there were so many stars. It was as if the sky had been blanketed by the Milky Way. A long line of mountaineers with their headlamps turned on were making their way up the Icefall as part of their acclimation training—preparation for summiting the mountain in the days, weeks, and even months ahead. They were early to bed and early to rise, often climbing in the middle of the night, because the ice warms up and becomes more unstable when the sun rises, making the morning and afternoon hours most susceptible to avalanches.

I stood there in the silence of the stars and prayed for their safety, while thanking the Lord for having brought me to Everest Base Camp.

My heart might not be as strong as I wanted, my neuromuscular system might be as poorly wired as a forty-year-old computer, but I had climbed the Himalayas.

My life was not over, not by a long stretch. My life was just beginning.

There was just one more thing I had to do: hike back down the damned thing.

I made it up here, I'll make it back down, I told myself. *Besides, it's all downhill from here. The worst of it is over.*

Little did I know, the worst was on its way.

CHAPTER 22:

RAPID DESCENT

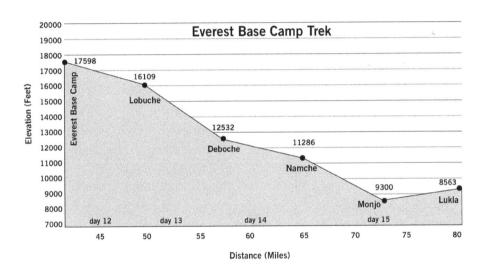

Efforts and courage are not enough without purpose and direction.

—John F. Kennedy

When I woke up the following morning, my tent—which had seemed like an icebox the night before—had turned into a sauna, trapping the warmth from the sun outside. I quickly arose from a small pool of sweat to reach for a drink, but all the water in my backpack was still frozen. I hustled to change out of my sweaty clothes and put on another pair of hiking pants and a T-shirt before heading down to breakfast with the group.

We had a lovely breakfast with our Chilean friends, which included French toast, good laughs, and some more man hugs, before we were forced to say our good-byes and head back down the mountain. I will never forget the brief time I spent with the Chilean expedition team on our trip, and we have remained in touch ever since.

▲▲ ▲▲ ▲▲

The order for our descent was more of the same, with Babu and Kendra traveling far up ahead while Kumar hiked in the back with me.

Although I was exhilarated to have reached Everest Base Camp, I realized only a part of the adventure was complete. It was equally important to navigate safely back down the mountain and return to my sister, and get home in one piece.

Since we had already accomplished the most difficult aspects of the hike with the elevation and acclimation, we could be more relaxed on the way down, savoring the serenity of the moment and capturing any Kodak moments we may have missed during our ascent while panting and gasping for air. While the hike down wouldn't necessarily be any easier, any safer, or any shorter with regards to distance, it would be much quicker. Descending, gravity helps pull your body downward, which can be more stressful on your legs and knees. However, there is no longer a need to acclimatize, as the body has already adjusted to the highest altitudes. This meant there would be less need to rest along the way, and quicker recovery times when we did break. We knew we could make it back to Lukla in half the time it had taken us to ascend to Base Camp.

We tentatively planned for our return hike to take five days, which would put us in Lukla the afternoon of April 25th. Each day we would cover practically double the distance we'd done coming up. On day one, we bypassed Gorak Shep, hiking from Base Camp all the way to Lobuche.

With each step, the fresh mountain air was easier to breathe. The five-mile journey of ups and downs lasted more than six hours, and the weather was perfect from start to finish. I wasn't able to remain in the

T-shirt I'd worn for breakfast, but the cold-weather gear was stored away, and all I needed was my hiking pants, an undershirt with a long-sleeve shirt over the top, and a buff around my neck to help protect against the sun and wind as we navigated along the trail.

I was excited about making it back home—not only to a warm and comfortable bed, but to my friends, family, and physicians, with whom I wanted to share my victory. I had done it; despite all the challenges and advisories not to even give it a try, I had done it. Furthermore, if I could do it, how many other people and patients with disabilities could achieve more than they realized?

My desire to inspire others grew greater with every step back down the mountain, and I began to dream of a different life—a life untethered to doctors and medical equipment. I wanted to reach out to all people with detours, obstacles, setbacks, and struggles in their path and demonstrate that more is possible in our futures than we might think. Just because our bodies are damaged, it doesn't mean our lives should be.

Many people, including some of my doctors, thought I was crazy to make this climb, but I'd done it. Perhaps if I hadn't been so concerned for my health, I wouldn't have made it. However, knowing how challenging it would be for my body, I had worked extra hard to prepare, and my preparation may have spared me the more severe complications that plagued others along the way. I knew altitude sickness could affect anyone to varying degrees, regardless of how healthy or prepared they might be—including my healthy sister, who had successfully accomplished the climb once before. I was fortunate it hadn't struck me.

I couldn't stop thinking about Chris. I'd spoken to her from Base Camp and knew she'd made it back to Kathmandu safely. I also knew she was an experienced nurse who had already seen a doctor and began to feel better immediately after her body was able to stabilize at a lower altitude. Still, her absence weighed heavily on my mind as I made my descent. We continued to speak daily for the rest of the trek, however—Kumar had a cell phone he let me use—and that offered me some sense of peace.

I was exhausted when we arrived in Lobuche, more due to the exhilaration of the previous days than from the trek itself. Upon our arrival, I took an afternoon nap, woke up for dinner with the group, and then went back to bed early in preparation for the following day.

While the accomplishment of making it to Everest Base Camp was the overall goal of my trip, meeting others throughout the journey provided additional meaning and memories behind that purpose. At breakfast, before leaving to head back down to Deboche, I had the opportunity to meet Pasang Lhamu Sherpa Akita, an impressive young woman who was the first-ever female mountaineering instructor in Nepal. She had summited Mount Everest back in 2007 and had the same name as the first Nepali woman to ever summit Mount Everest back in 1993. She had spent a lot of time in the United States, summiting Mount Rainier several times while she was there, and spoke very good English. On this trip she was guiding a fine gentleman named Chris who had grown up in Denver, gone to school in Chicago, and moved to Russia a few years earlier.

Like other climbers and guides along the way, Pasang Lhamu and Chris were very supportive of my ambitions and wanted to hear all about my voyage. It was a refreshing visit. Other than broken conversations with Kumar, I hadn't really spoken to anyone since leaving Base Camp. I realized that on this trip, very much like my difficult days of my health recovery, the people I thought would support me weren't always there. At times, the encouragement came from those I least expected.

▲▲ ▲▲ ▲▲

Hiking back to Deboche, the trails were sparse of people, which gave me plenty of time to reflect on all I had just gone through. After spending a night at Base Camp and meeting some climbers who would soon put their lives on the line hoping to summit Mount Everest, the return through Thokla Pass had a far different feel. There were no horses, guides, or teams of hikers on this day—just plenty of quiet, a gorgeous cloud cover, and a gentle breeze. It literally and metaphorically seemed like a ghost town.

The day was beautiful, the air was fresh, and the nine miles to Deboche went by fast. Before long, we happened upon the fallen bridge we had seen on the way up. This time, I was no longer in awe of the destruction and annoyed about going around; instead, I was humbled by the environment and at peace that no one was injured when the bridge collapsed during the off-season.

▲▲   ▲▲   ▲▲

The lovely weather continued as we made our way from Deboche to Namche. The distance to travel was much shorter, only six miles, but the grade of decline was far more substantial, and by this point my sore feet were turning swollen and blistery. It was most evident at night before bed and first thing in the morning. There was nothing to do but rest, and that would be done when I made it back to Lukla.

Unlike our visit on the way up, the weather was gorgeous as we passed through the village of Tengboche; the monastery and the colors were bright and the backdrop of the mountains was majestic. I felt full of peace and contentment. I was so happy to be on my way back, so gratified by the simple solitude of the mountains. My mind was in such a patient and positive place.

Given the lower altitude and amazing weather, there were many more people on the trails on this day, and we came across several animals. I stand at five-foot-eleven and weigh approximately two hundred pounds, and I was amazed when we encountered men nearly half my size carrying four times their weight upon their backs without breaking a sweat. The impossible-to-ignore pink flowers we passed along the hillside seemed to jump out on the trail. The wind was blowing hard, and it blocked out all other noise as I crossed one bridge after another.

When we came upon an extensively winding portion of the trail that was largely flat, I felt compelled to sit and savor the pure satisfaction I was feeling.

"Kumar," I said, "can we stop for a minute?"

"Is everything all right, Rob, sir?"

"I'm great!" I responded. "I just want to sit here and take a picture."

Just as I sat on a boulder at the side of the path with my legs dangling high above the trees below, my sister called. Kumar answered and handed me the phone.

"How are you doing?" Chris asked.

"I've never been better," I replied. "Today is amazing!"

"What do you mean?" she asked, sounding surprised. "What's going on?"

"Nothing," I said, "it's just a beautiful day and I'm happy to be enjoying it. I wish you were here; how are you feeling?"

She said she was feeling good, not having any ill effects from the mountain sickness, and had begun to explore Kathmandu while waiting for me to return safely.

After we hung up, I just enjoyed the peaceful view with Kumar, the tranquility of the moment rejuvenating my strength. Then we continued on.

After another half-mile of the bends and turns along the side of the mountains, we came to a gentleman sitting on a chain in the middle of the trail. His name was Lobsang Lama, and people in the area called him "The Grandfather." Between the weather and annual hikers, the trails needed proper maintenance and cleaning, and The Grandfather was always working to raise money to assist in rehabbing the trails. I donated some of my Nepalese rupee to him before we continued our hike.

Before long, we were coming down on Namche Bazaar with its colorful buildings and shops. We arrived at the hotel fairly early in the afternoon, and today, unlike most days, I didn't need to rest. After dropping my things in the room, I went out to explore the town for a few hours and purchased postcards, a map of the area, hiking pants, a thick fleece hiking jacket, and a T-shirt. I was so happy with the trip, and now I had the memorabilia to serve as a reminder.

That evening after dinner, I had another remarkable encounter. Jamling Tenzing Norgay—the son of Sherpa Tenzing Norgay who, with Sir Edmund Hillary, was the first to reach the summit of Mount Everest—was in Namche to lead a group of young Indian women on a trek. Jamling had first scaled Everest's peak himself during the fateful climb of 1996 when a deadly blizzard hit and killed eight people.

I spent a couple of amazing hours chatting with Jamling and the head of the ice doctors, Ang Dorjee Sherpa (who also happened to be the husband of the woman who owned Hotel Namche, where we were staying). The two men were as kind and gracious as they were fascinating. And for me, the meeting was symbolic. Consider how I began this amazing experience: meeting Peter Hillary and learning about Mount Everest and Nepal on my trip to Antarctica five years earlier had started it all. Now I was able to place a bookend to that experience. After going through all my surgeries and having a brush with death in 2011, working toward my recovery in 2012, and now embarking on this journey to put an exclamation point on my recovery in 2015, I was able to meet Jamling Norgay. I don't think many people can say they've met the two great mountaineering sons of the two legendary mountaineers who were the first to ever hike to the very top of the tallest mountain in the world!

▲▲ ▲▲ ▲▲

The morning of April 24th, after setting out after breakfast, I practically ran back down the mountain, I was so excited about making it back to Lukla and finishing the trek. Hiking back down the mountain, however, isn't any safer than hiking up; you still must be careful with your movements. There were several times where I was hurrying so much that I almost lost my balance—and at one point, I *did* lose my balance.

I fell as I was going down some steep steps and trying to avoid some other hikers on the trail. I could have been patient and waited for the area to clear, but instead I tried to pass along the side. As I took some large steps down, I began to lose my balance and easily could have fallen over the side of the mountain and been killed. Thankfully, I was able to grab hold of a tree and was quickly rescued by Kumar and others nearby.

That moment was a wake-up call—a reminder that just because I'd made it to the top didn't mean the danger was over. In fact, more people die descending the mountain than they do ascending it.

"Be careful," Kumar cautioned me. "It's slippery."

"Absolutely," I said.

"Walk slowly," he said. "You walk too fast. You maybe fall and die."

Once I slowed down, I again was able to appreciate all that was around me, including a blind man hiking up the mountain with a guide as we passed by. Watching a man without sight make the ascent both humbled me and gave me an extra sense of pride in what I had done. I was now one in a long line of people with disabilities who had scaled mountains, both literally and figuratively.

▲▲ ▲▲ ▲▲

On April 24th, after only four days of hiking downhill, we made it to Lukla. We had planned to sleep in Phakding that night and get to Lukla the next day, but I was so excited to reach Lukla we decided to double the distance on our last day and push through. By late afternoon, we had reached Lukla, the place where our trek began.

In total, we had hiked more than one hundred miles back and forth through the Himalayas, the equivalent of more than 200,000 steps. We had altered our altitude by more than 22,000 feet during the two-week journey up and down the foothills of Sagarmatha National Park.

My body had taken a beating in the mountains, and I was utterly exhausted. My hands and feet were a combination of blistery, discolored, and swollen, my legs and back were aching and sore, my face and ears were red from sunburn, and I had a painful split in my upper and lower lips due to the dry mountain air and wind.

Still, it had been the experience of a lifetime, and I was ecstatic. I had no way of knowing that in less than twenty-four hours, I would endure an event that would make the trip even more unforgettable.

CHAPTER 23:

THE EARTH SHAKES

When you reach the end of your rope, tie a knot and hang on.
—Franklin D. Roosevelt

On our last night in the mountains together, our team met for a celebratory dinner and welcomed our shy porter to join the group. It was a simple get-together, yet it had a special vibe. The guides and porter weren't accustomed to sharing meals with trekkers. During our two-week journey, Kumar and Babu had almost always sat at a separate table once Chris, Kendra, and I had been taken care of, and we had rarely even seen the porter. But this night was different; it was special.

As I sat there looking around at the people gathered at that dinner, I thought about how far I had come, and the epic climax at Everest Base Camp. I couldn't have done it without them, and in the two weeks we had spent trekking through the mountains together, we had created an indestructible bond. This thought led me to reflect on how each individual in my life—all the doctors and nurses and family and friends— had played a vital role in bringing my dream to fruition, and how their encouragement and even discouragement had fueled my energy along the way.

After dinner, we relaxed with an Everest beer and even tried some Everest whiskey—which was much stronger than anything I'd ever tried back home—with Kumar, Babu, and our new porter friend. It was a nice evening, just what we needed to end our trip. There was no rush to get anywhere, no thinking about a grueling trek we'd have to make in the morning, just pure enjoyment.

▲▲   ▲▲   ▲▲

Early the next morning, we woke to a gray and dreary fog and moderate to high winds swirling amongst the flags. We thanked our hosts and said good-bye to Babu, who, after being away from his wife and infant daughter for several weeks, would be walking back to his home—a trek of two days—since there were no roads for driving in the small villages nestled in the mountains. It seemed like a heavy burden to me, but that was the life of a guide.

Then Kumar escorted us to the airport, where our early flight kept getting delayed due to the weather. Hanging out for a couple of hours at the airport was actually rather fun; I had this huge sense of accomplishment and pride and had some great conversations with other hikers who'd traveled in the mountains. I was so happy that I found myself getting excited over the silliest things, like buying refrigerator magnets or cookies from the kiosk.

Eventually, our flight was canceled altogether, and Kumar brought us back to our teahouse in Lukla for lunch and to await further word.

"How about that?" I said. "The trip is ending the same way it began. What is it about me and airplanes? Just when I'm most excited to get on one, I can't!"

I had spent so much of my life getting angry when things didn't turn out the way I'd planned—breaking my back and not getting a football scholarship, developing heart problems and then muscular dystrophy, falling in love and having it not work out, even missing a flight to India. Now, after having climbed to Everest Base Camp, something inside me had changed. I had learned that everything did work out in the end. I had gone to college, I was still strong and active, I was still hopeful to find love, and I'd still made it to Nepal. I thought back to that sermon on detours and smiled. This time, instead of being angry that things weren't turning out as I'd planned, I felt content. It was just another detour—another unexpected turn of events that could lead to anything.

I was also quite exhausted, however. My body was shot, my back was hurting, my nose was peeling, and my feet were swollen and had turned red and purple. I just wanted to go to sleep.

"Let's go teahouse for lunch," Kumar suggested. "I will check to see when plane will leave."

Hauling our luggage, we returned to the teahouse we'd stayed in the night before, a nice little place nestled right into the side of a mountain.

"No plane," the woman at the teahouse told us. "Maybe afternoon or tomorrow."

All that rushing to get to Lukla as soon as possible, and now all we could do was stay there and wait.

There weren't many people in the teahouse, just Kendra and me, Kumar, a middle-aged couple from Massachusetts and their guide, and the husband and wife who owned the teahouse. We had just finished lunch and were sitting around talking, wondering whether we'd be able to fly back to Kathmandu and see my sister later that afternoon, when, at 11:56 a.m. precisely, a loud, long rumbling sound came out of nowhere and engulfed us as the ground and everything around us began to shake.

During those first few paralyzing seconds, Kendra and I stared at each other like deer in headlights, dazed about what was happening and how to respond. Even as my mind was able to process that it was an earthquake I was experiencing, I had no idea what to do; my only reaction was to grasp the shaking table before me, as if that somehow might protect us. The powerful pulsations and sounds of the earthquake made me feel like I was standing on a suspension bridge while large semi-trailer trucks whizzed by, vibrating every square inch of the structure.

The couple who owned the teahouse desperately tried to save the dishes that were falling from the shelves. As I rose from the table to assist the couple in saving their possessions, Kumar pleaded with me to sit down. I followed his advice and returned to the table in silence while my mind tried to make sense of all that was happening.

"Let's get the hell out of here," the man from Massachusetts yelled above the rumbling sound.

"No, stay here," his guide said. "It's safer."

He was right—we were pressed against the mountain, and the buildings were practically piled right on top of each other. It was much less safe outside, where there was more that could come crashing down upon us.

The rumbling and shaking must have lasted for a good minute and a half, although it felt like forever. Then, just as suddenly as it had started, it stopped: the thunderous sounds from the earthquake were silenced. But they were quickly replaced by screams and cries throughout the village.

Through the windows, we could see people scurrying from buildings and parents scooping up babies and children and pressing them close to their chests as they rushed for safety. We remained still, realizing that running into the street would put us in the danger zone and that staying in place would be our best choice.

I felt exactly as I had when my defibrillator had gone off back in 2011. I had been told it could go off, but there was no way to prepare for the shock when it did. When it went off again and again, I knew I had to stay calm; I knew I couldn't panic. I had to assess the situation and give myself a moment to think clearly.

Through my years of surgeries and heart incidents and even all my years of competitive sports, I have learned that the first response most people have during a crisis is to feel an immediate need to do something, anything. But then, not knowing what to do, we end up spinning our wheels and often make a situation worse. Inaction helps to calm us, and this was one of those times when I had to stay calm.

Everyone in the teahouse was deadly silent. We were all looking at one another, waiting for what seemed like an eternity. Slowly, in a surreal unfolding of time and space, we began to collect ourselves. The man from Massachusetts, clearly frightened, began swearing. The owners of the teahouse scrambled to retrieve what few dishes hadn't broken, but most of the plates and bowls were shattered, just like the couple's livelihood.

"Are you okay?" I asked the owner and his wife.

They assured me they were.

I checked with Kumar and the other couple, and when it was clear that none of us had been injured and the earth remained still, I ventured outside to see if I could assist the people screaming and crying in the streets.

Everything was a mess. There was debris everywhere. A combination of rubble from the mountains and buildings blanketed the one road cutting through the middle of town. Colorful clothes and scarves I had seen being sold as souvenirs outside the shop next door were strewn across the street, and a dark cloud of dust lingered in the air. Babies and children were wailing, their mothers trying to comfort them. Some people were walking, holding their heads or arms, injured and bleeding. Others hadn't been so fortunate, crushed by falling rocks from the hillside above.

Farther up in the mountains, I knew it had to be worse. There would be avalanches, falling rocks, and mudslides. Climbers could easily have been buried and crushed or fallen to their deaths. We could have been among them if we were still up there like we were initially scheduled to be. I wondered if the Chilean team, Melissa Arnot, and all the others I'd met during the trek were safe.

That thought brought me to a sudden realization: Chris was in Kathmandu. What had happened there? There were so many buildings, so much greater potential for injury. Was she okay? I had to reach her, but all power and cell reception had been lost during the upheaval.

The scene around me brought me back to reality. People were already trying to clean up the mess, trying to restore their lives. Everyone was helping everyone, and there was nothing to do but try to pitch in. Staying close to the teahouse, I helped pick up signs, clothes, and other items that had fallen to the street during the quake. Unfortunately, little more could be done by hand.

After spending an hour or so aiding in the streets with the futile cleanup effort, I returned to the teahouse, where no one felt safe enough to go to their rooms. We knew there could be aftershocks and wanted to be with each other when they hit.

The electricity and cell phone service were restored around seven o'clock in the evening. After numerous attempts to reach Chris through the network overload, I was finally able to get through to her. She'd been at the Yak & Yeti for a conference on tattoos and body piercings she'd decided to attend. When the earth began to rumble, everyone had made a mad dash for the door and she'd been knocked to the ground and trampled over by a stampede of pierced and body-painted people. She said she was okay. Only after she returned to the States would she discover she had three fractured ribs.

We were so relieved to hear each other's voice.

"It was a 7.8 on the Richter scale, Robby," she told me, "and they say there's going to be another one around nine o'clock and it's supposed to be even worse."

This was the first I was hearing about predictions for aftershocks, since we had no access to information up there.

The news was terrifying. If there was another, even worse one coming, when would it hit and what would it do?

After Chris and I had hung up, I was faced with a dilemma: Should I tell the others, or would that only frighten them?

After I told Kendra and Kumar, we agreed the news had to be shared with the other patrons of the teahouse. I walked over and spoke with the owner and his wife, the couple from Massachusetts and then another couple who'd been hiking and had joined us. The news left us all on edge, but as happens in emergencies, we bonded in our shared fear and relief that, so far, we had survived.

Nine o'clock came and went, and there was no other earthquake. Eventually, after midnight, we all went to our rooms to get some sleep. It was a restless sleep, though. The slightest sound jolted me awake and for minutes afterward I'd lie in silence, listening for any indication that the big one had arrived. Thank goodness, it never did.

Still, I couldn't truly relax until I was back home and out of harm's way.

CHAPTER 24:

REUNITED AGAIN

Love and compassion are necessities, not luxuries. Without
them, humanity cannot survive.

—Dalai Lama

Waking up the next morning was like waking from a terrible
dream. I was confused about what was real and what was an
illusion. I had worn my day clothes and hiking boots to bed
and left my packed bags next to the door, just in case there was another
earthquake and we needed to evacuate suddenly in the middle of the
night, all of which made me feel even more discombobulated.

Kendra and I joined the others from the teahouse in the main room
for breakfast, just as a procession of somber-looking villagers passed by
on the main road outside the window. In groups of four, they were carrying wooden boxes on their shoulders, the bodies of the earthquake
victims inside. Others were spraying grains of rice as they all walked
down the road toward the airport.

The clouds from the day before had lifted and the dust and debris that had filled the air in the aftermath of the quake settled in the stead of a clear blue sky full of helicopters flying to and from the airport with victims from the mountains in need of evacuation. We walked to the airport, which had become a staging area for the wounded, and watched with hundreds of others as people on stretchers were carried off the helicopters that continued to come in. After the earthquake, a deadly avalanche had obliterated Base Camp, creating the deadliest disaster in the history of Mount Everest. Many had been killed and even more injured.

Medical personnel waited at the airport to triage the victims being flown in from the mountains. A thumbs-up meant they were critically injured but hopeful, and then they were transferred to an airplane on the other side of the asphalt for the next flight back to Kathmandu for care. A thumbs-down meant they were critically injured and probably wouldn't survive the flight, so they were brought inside the building for immediate attention. A black tag signified the individual had died, and the body was placed in a developing row along the side of the building.

It was a dreadful scene, and all I could do was look and wonder about the circumstances of the victims being carried and the emotionless decisions that needed to be made identifying who could be saved and who couldn't. After a few hours where all I could do was watch in a daze, I headed back to the teahouse for lunch and an update.

Kumar waited as I arrived at the door; my sister was on the phone once again.

"Robby," she said. "Are you ready to go?"

"Yes!" I exclaimed. "What's up?"

"Go back to the airport; there is a helicopter waiting, but you have to leave now!"

Jiban had been working feverishly back in Kathmandu to secure us an emergency helicopter to take us from Lukla back to Kathmandu. Our bags were packed, so after exchanging warm good-byes with those we'd shared our day and night of terror with, we hurried to the airport. Kumar led Kendra and me to a helipad off to the side of the runway where the aircraft was still and the pilot waited.

Around 1:00 p.m., just twenty-five hours after the harrowing earthquake, we were evacuated.

The forty-five-minute escape from Lukla by helicopter was completely different than the exhilarating flight we'd taken to get there. Shortly after liftoff, it became very rainy and we passed through many dark, turbulent clouds. When there was a break in the clouds, we were able to somewhat survey the villages below, though we were too high up to really discern what was going on.

As we began to approach Kathmandu, however, we descended enough to see some of what was happening on the ground below. It was a surreal sight. The city had been hit hard. There were collapsed roofs and crumbled buildings. Many of the people we could see had flocked to wide-open spaces. Once we landed, we learned that a 6.7 magnitude aftershock had hit while we were still in the air, causing even more devastation and destruction and, most of all, fear and panic. That's why the people had gathered in those open areas—it's the safest place to be in the midst of an earthquake, away from falling debris and rocks.

I carried our bags off the helicopter and walked with the pilot and Kendra to a waiting area nearby. Jiban showed up in the passenger seat of an airport security truck about fifteen minutes later. After loading our bags and exchanging a quick hello, we drove across the airport grounds to the parking lot, passing many aircraft and soldiers along the way who had flown in from nearby countries like India to assist. Many of them were bringing in aid for the wounded and supplies for the people of Nepal. Outside the gates were thousands of people waiting in line, seeking a flight back home. It was a chaotic mess.

Jiban escorted us to the parking lot where his personal truck was parked, and there was Chris. I'd never been so happy to see my sister in all my life. We embraced tightly and I was relieved to see that she appeared fine; she even teased me about the beard I had grown over the two-week hike.

We transferred our luggage into the new truck and set off, this time back to the Yak & Yeti, where we'd spent our first couple of nights in Nepal. On the drive back from the airport to the hotel, the streets and alleys looked like a war zone. Buildings that had been reduced to rubble stood right next to buildings that appeared untouched. Ancient monasteries, along with grand statues of Buddhas, had been destroyed. Streets were blocked off, and Jiban patiently took alternative routes.

"Detours," he explained.

I smiled. "That's all right, Jiban. I don't mind detours anymore."

I would often come to reflect in the days and months after the earthquake upon the many detours during the journey that may have saved our lives—starting with the cancelation of the India leg of the trip. Had it not been for that flight snafu, we would have started our hike two days later. Then we'd decided not to acclimatize an extra day in Gorak Shep, and Kendra and I had gained yet one more day when we'd pushed through Phakding all the way back to Lukla on the final day of the hike. Those four days and nights may have made a difference between life and death. The dumb luck or divine intervention in the narrow escape was not lost on me, and I was thankful to be alive. Had we not reached Base Camp earlier than scheduled or descended so quickly, we could have been incapacitated by the earthquake, avalanche, or mudslides that had killed twenty-four people and injured more than three times as many at Base Camp alone, and had left hundreds of other climbers and hikers stranded in the mountains.

When we finally reached the Yak & Yeti, it wasn't the safe haven I had hoped for. It had been hit pretty hard, and guests weren't being allowed back in their rooms. All the visitors were gathered outside, where we spent the rest of the day hanging out and waiting, with nothing to do but talk about the terrifying experience we'd survived and wonder what would come next.

The atmosphere was a mix of weary excitement at having survived such an event and tension as we continued to wait for the big one we were told could come but never did. By nightfall, it had begun to rain, and we still couldn't return to our rooms, so we slept outside in sleeping bags and makeshift combinations of pillows and blankets under the Himalayan stars, covering ourselves with whatever we could to stay dry. I didn't sleep well, and my back and feet hurt more than ever, but after all I had been through leading up to the trek to Base Camp—and now, after witnessing the destruction caused by this earthquake—I was thankful to be alive.

With all those fears my doctors had about my heart or muscles not being able to withstand the hike, it wasn't my body that had ultimately threatened me, it was Mother Nature herself. I thought about how suddenly everything had changed when the rumbling began. People who had been happy and healthy and alive one minute were critically injured or dead the next. Realizing how instantly life can end—not just for those with serious health problems but for anyone—humbled me and brought my own broken body into perspective.

I was no different than anyone else. We all live with death at our backs, never knowing when it will take us.

The following afternoon, we received an update from the ambassador of the hotel. We had gotten little to no sleep, and we were restless. After the update, a take-charge type of man spoke above the crowd.

His name was Shawn Dawson, and, I later learned, he was the eighth person to complete the Seven Summits challenge. Inspiring from afar and genuine up close, Shawn had also founded an organization called the Dream Mountains Foundation, which, in connection with his realization of climbing the Seven Summits, supported seven charities. He was there leading a group of trekkers from Ottawa, Canada, named the Dream Team.

They were a friendly group doing their best to tolerate the situation. After spending more than a year training and raising funds for this event, their dream of hiking to the base camp of the tallest mountain in the world had turned into an impenetrable trail of rubble.

I could relate to this fine group of Canadians. I knew what it was like to come so far and then have to face the fact that, because of circumstances beyond your control, you may not be able to reach your goal. I was painfully familiar with the idea of having to come up with a new target to strive for. Despite the tension of the overall situation, however, in the next forty-eight hours, we became close friends. Together, we ate, drank, talked, laughed, and cried, but most notably, we lived.

We were still unable to sleep in our rooms that night, but the hotel allowed us to dodge the elements and sleep in the lobby. With rows of people lying on the floor draped in sleeping bags and extra pillows and blankets supplied by the hotel, the scene was eerie, an unpleasant reminder of the bodies that were lying next to one another in Lukla. The

TV was on, and many were glued to the news for updates and statistics on the aftershocks that continued to take place. In less than a month after the initial quake there would be more than 450 of them greater than 4.0 on the Richter scale, including the 6.7 that occurred the day before and a 7.3 on May 12th.

The hotel clock made a noise, a small clicking sound, on the hour. At two o'clock in the morning, when people were ready to pass out, on top of the clicking sound, some birds started chirping nearby. One of the patrons, startled by the noise, shot up from the ground and screamed.

"It's an earthquake!" he yelled, creating an instant panic.

"It's here!" another person shouted, creating a chain reaction of people screaming and scrambling for the doors in fear for their lives.

"It's okay!" a hotel employee explained. "It's just the clock and some birds."

Everyone was on edge and terrified of the next quake. Although nothing came, it was déjà vu over and over throughout the evening. Those who were scared reacted in a way that made it impossible for the calm to sleep, and we all lay there, awake and exhausted, until the morning light.

The transition between night and day became a blur during the two days we slept outside in the elements and on the ground floor of the hotel. On day two, the hotel was flooded by reporters who were flying in from all over the world, including a British journalist from Hong Kong who worked for *The New York Times* and came to the hotel looking to interview survivors. As one of the first people to make it back from the mountains who'd survived the earthquake, I was asked for an interview, and I suggested they speak to my sister as well.

Quite often, we don't realize the potential impact our actions and words can have on others. I wasn't trying to be a hero or anyone special, I was just trying to survive like everyone else. Nevertheless, the experience and situation made me unique, and suddenly what I had to say mattered.

Finally, on the night of April 28th, my final night in Kathmandu, we were given permission to stay in our rooms at our own risk. I couldn't have been more relieved to finally cradle my excruciating back on a proper mattress, the first real mattress I'd slept on in two weeks. I took the opportunity to shower for the first time in days and shave for the first time in weeks. For the five minutes the water splashed down on my face and body, I was in utopia. The concerns had faded, the worries were gone, and I was recharged.

Departing Kathmandu, Chris, Kendra, and I were all on separate flights. Since I had signed up to participate in the final run of Disney World's Expedition Everest Challenge, a fun race and obstacle course through Animal Kingdom, I had booked a flight to Orlando and would make it back to Chicago from there. When I'd planned the race it had seemed like a great way to end a phenomenal trip, but after all I had been through, it seemed preposterous—even more so after witnessing the devastation of Kathmandu.

We spent our final day in Nepal walking around the city, our first time leaving the hotel since the earthquake. The destruction on the streets was astonishing: Broken glass was everywhere, inside the shops and on the sidewalks and streets. The whole city was in rubble, as if it had been bombed. All the parks had been converted to camps, and those without homes had settled into tents.

The strength and determination of the Nepalese people really impressed me. They were still trying to make a living, and they continued to sell things to tourists while trying to repair the damage to their shops. They were laughing and joking as if nothing had happened.

If a disaster like that occurred in Chicago, people would be helping each other out, but the darker side of humanity would also emerge. There would be all kinds of looting and who knows what kind of conflict might result. In Kathmandu, though, there was no looting. Everyone took care of each other, and the spirit of cooperation and mutual protection was amazing. I knew I would forever cherish not just the climb I'd achieved but also the Nepalese people; they had taught me a lesson in patience and human kindness.

Later that evening, Jiban and Chris took me back to the airport for my flight. After more hugs and good-byes, I flew back to the US alone.

After more than twenty-two hours of air travel with stops in Qatar and Philadelphia, I arrived in Orlando sick as a dog. I had developed a terrible case of bronchitis, and on top of that the skin on my hands and feet were peeling off. I could barely walk.

I was in no shape to run five feet, let alone a 5K race. However, with everything I had endured, I was ready to see it through. I rented a car and went to a friend's house for the evening before heading to the race the following morning. Although I wasn't about to participate, I had to go; I had to see Everest, the Disney version.

After I picked up my shirt and pins for the race, it was time to go home.

I changed my flight, went back to the airport a day early, and got on the next plane home to Chicago.

I was sick and exhausted, but I'd done what I'd set out to do. The experience had truly been bittersweet, and I was utterly happy.

I'd made it.

EPILOGUE

The 7.8-magnitude earthquake I survived in Nepal was the worst natural disaster to hit the region since 1934. More than 9,000 people were killed—twenty-four of them at Everest Base Camp. Hundreds of climbers were stranded in the mountains for days and weeks before being helicoptered to safety. More than 20,000 people were critically injured in the region, and hundreds of thousands were left homeless. That year, 2015, was the first since 1974 that not a single person was able to summit Mount Everest.

In the end, more than 700,000 homes were destroyed throughout the region, mostly in villages, with another 200,000 left in need of repair. The overall economic damage was estimated around $10 billion, which is more than half of Nepal's gross domestic product. Rescue efforts to reach those trapped in the mountains lasted for weeks, and reconstruction efforts would take years—a huge blow to a country that was already one of the poorest in the world.

I had never anticipated such a calamity could strike during my Nepal trip, a trip I had taken to celebrate my medical recovery. To suddenly have the earth itself shake so violently was a startling reminder of how precarious life can be for us all.

When I first learned of my heart problems and had to get a pacemaker/defibrillator, I was angry and scared. Then, when I found out I had muscular dystrophy like my dad, I wondered how much more I would have to endure. A part of me felt cheated that after having worked so hard to maintain a healthy and honorable lifestyle, I'd ended up with a damaged body and a heart so weak that I needed a computer and battery in my chest to keep it working.

I worried I might never live to marry and have children, much less grandchildren. I resented having to spend so much time fighting for what I wanted, debating with doctors, insurance companies, and employers, enduring tests, and wearing uncomfortable monitors.

I also struggled with how other people viewed my challenges to move and participate. Some would argue that I was fine when I labored to stand or criticize me when I sought to rest. I didn't have braces, crutches, or a wheelchair that would make my disability obvious. Instead, I had an invisible disease: an irregular heartbeat, pain, and fatigue that no one else could see yet were still limiting my daily abilities.

It has taken time to process all that has happened and move forward. I don't blame anyone or anything for my difficult times, and I am grateful for the love and encouragement I've received from family, friends, and countless other supporters.

I have also had a fantastic team of doctors behind me, and I've learned that the physicians best suited to help me are the ones who welcome my feedback and answer my questions. By working together, we've always found the best path toward my recovery.

For me, self-advocacy has been the best approach to staying as happy and healthy as possible. I've questioned my doctors and taken an active role in my own healthcare, discussing and researching my disorders and potential treatment options. And although I've always listened to my doctors and respected their medical advice, I've never simply done what I was told without understanding why I was doing it. Most important, I've never made a decision about any surgeries, medications, healthcare, or courses of recovery without making sure I was informed about the risks and benefits of each.

None of this has come easily, of course. There were many points along the way where I felt isolated and alone and considered giving up.

With an open mind and quest for knowledge to overcome these challenges, however, I reached out for help and found strength in others. I joined groups and discovered the many networks of people suffering from similar conditions who could appreciate and understand what I was going through. Through them, I learned a great deal about the range of possible treatments and how to live with my disorders. I also made wonderful friends along the way. Now, I regularly attend various conferences on heart disease and muscular dystrophy, where I share my knowledge and Mount Everest story as a way to demonstrate to others with medical conditions that if they push themselves, they can still achieve their dreams.

My doctors first thought I was crazy to attempt the hike to Mount Everest Base Camp, but they were proud (and relieved) when I returned triumphant and safe. It was their job to err on the side of caution and discourage me from making a foolish decision, but by training and testing myself, I grew stronger. I learned that no matter what my limitations, I did not need to sit on the couch doing nothing and let life pass me by. I could still enjoy living my life and pursue an active lifestyle so long as I continued to set realistic and achievable goals and challenge myself accordingly. Everyone is different, and we all have different needs and wants. My personality is competitive, and I will always strive to better myself. Though I struggle physically at times, emotionally I feel stronger today than I did on the day I completed my mission and reached Everest Base Camp.

Many of the hardships I've endured in my life are a direct result of some of the bad decisions I've made along the way, but those obstacles have always become opportunities for improvement. In fact, I would argue that some of the ambition, drive, and success I've had is the result of what I've been able to endure. I have also learned from this experience that it is important not to dwell on the past and to pursue the happiness that seems unattainable at times.

This entire experience has also taught me to never give up. I was reminded of this lesson in 2016 when, after victory had eluded them for 108 years, my favorite baseball team, the Chicago Cubs, won the World Series, a triumph I wish my grandpa and father could have seen. Through determination, hard work, and persistence, the Cubs proved anything can happen and that there is always hope.

Though I will continue to battle my condition with vigor and tenacity, I look forward to the calmer and less dramatic days that lie ahead. My goals for the future are far more modest than climbing to the base camp of the tallest mountain in the world, but I will continue to push myself and keep busy.

At the time of writing this book, I have been to forty-five of the fifty states in the US and have seen a home game in every Major League Baseball stadium. Now, it's my goal to visit the remaining five states and attend a football game in every NFL stadium. I have visited all seven continents and cruised four of the five oceans, and I will continue to travel. I still hope to visit India and the Taj Mahal someday, and if I do so, I'll get the visa ahead of time! I also intend to visit South Africa and hike to Machu Picchu in the not-so-distant future.

When I first came up with the concept of putting a book together, I hoped for a happy ending to my story where I could share about my falling in love and finding the woman of my dreams. Since my health struggles are largely related to my heart, I felt that finding the right woman to share my heart with would be the perfect fairy-tale conclusion to my story, and for years I searched and waited for my happy ending. As time went on, however, I began to put all my energies into my healthcare and lifestyle, and as a result, I was not always available to give my full attention to a woman in my life, however deserving she might be. Now that I've matured and realize many of the limitations I must live with and the possibilities for an exciting life that remain, I am ready to be the Romeo to my Juliet. One lesson I have learned, however, is that it is not necessary to find a partner in order to have a full and wonderful life. I'm confident the right woman for me is out there, and we'll find each other when the time is right.

In the meantime, my life has been a blessing. I'm going to continue to live it—to handle every obstacle, manage every detour, and set sensible and attainable goals to move toward. I can't always command what happens, but I am in charge of how I respond. The happy ending to my story doesn't have to be falling in love with a partner; the happy ending is continuing to get back up after being knocked down and loving life. No matter what life throws my way, I am still in control of who I am, what I do, and where I go, and I will be forever strong!

ACKNOWLEDGMENTS

There are many people who have played an important role in helping me reach the point I have gotten to with my health and recovery, and they deserve some special thanks. First and foremost, I want to recognize my late mom and dad. Without their love and support through the years, I never would have turned into the man I am today.

As a result of my battles with chronic heart and muscle disease, I have crossed paths with countless dedicated medical professionals. While all of my physicians have played an important role in my care and well-being, there are three I want to name specifically: Dr. Melissa Ferarro-Borgida, who was the first to dive in to my heart issue and essentially save my life; Dr. Thomas Bump, who has been the kindest and most supportive provider I could ever hope to work with; and Dr. Elizabeth McNally, who worked with me to find a safer way to pursue my goals, even when she didn't agree that I should.

I also have to thank Dr. John Day and The Stanford Neuromuscular Disorders Team for welcoming me to their myotonic dystrophy information meetings, as well as Dr. Ian Law and the Pediatric Cardiology Team out of University of Iowa Hospital for their invitation to participate in the

Young Hearts with ICDs annual conference. Both physicians and organizations provided encouragement before, during, and especially after my trip to Everest Base Camp.

I have worked with and endorsed several organizations, but there is one in my life that has shined above the rest. The Muscular Dystrophy Association (MDA) has had a tremendous impact on me, both through the connections it has provided and the assistance it has given since both my father and I were diagnosed with muscular dystrophy.

For helping me to train and prepare for the hike up to Base Camp, I must thank Dr. Mike McCahill of McCahill Chiropractic as well as Jennifer Strickland of Life Time Fitness. Dr. McCahill introduced me to TRX, while personal trainer Jennifer Strickland pushed me to a fitness level I no longer knew I could reach.

Putting that training into action couldn't have been done without moral support and planning to help make my dream become a reality. For that, a special thanks to my sister Chris Griffin, who, after swearing she would never do it again, attempted the trek to Everest Base Camp a second time to accompany her baby brother. Also, thanks to Jiban Ghimire of Shangri-La Nepal, who handled all the arrangements for the trek and helped me endure two disasters in the mountains of Nepal.

Though I say the trek itself has been the hardest thing I've ever done on purpose, the writing of this book is a close second; I'd like to extend a special shout-out to Janice Harper and Elise McIntosh for bearing with me and helping to make this publication a reality.

I would like to thank Glen Rodrigue, Alan Close, and Holly Morrell, who were among the first I met after being diagnosed with heart disease and remain key figures in my life today.

Finally, it's important for me to express my gratitude to Diana and Kathy, whose immeasurable love and kindness helped me overcome limitless hurdles.

There are simply too many people to thank all of them by name, but I am grateful for every single person who has played a part in my journey. I am deeply humbled by each of the people who visited me during my hospital stays, as well as those who called and reached out with messages of support when I needed them most. I am grateful to those who planted seeds of inspiration by sharing their experiences and driving me to pursue more. I'm even motivated by those people who hindered my progress, forcing me to fight even harder.

If I could physically reach out through the pages of this book and give you each a big hug, I would. From the bottom of my heart, I offer a sincere thank-you to everyone past, present, and future who has lifted me up during the difficult times, promoted me during the good times, and encouraged me to be a better person.

ABOUT THE AUTHOR

ROB BESECKER is an author, inspirational speaker, and health-care professional who spends much of his time advocating for hospice care patients and their families. His passion for healthcare and help-ing others live their best lives comes from his own experience living with chronic heart ailments and muscular dystrophy, and a relentless drive to squeeze the most value out of each day. A global adventurist and semi-professional bucket list checker, Besecker has visited all seven con-tinents, the Great Pyramids, and the Great Wall of China. In this trium-phant personal memoir, he shares the fascinating story of the physical and mental challenges that led him on a journey of incredible adventure and self-discovery—from months spent in hospital beds, questioning his chances of survival, to leaping toward his biggest challenge yet—a hiking expedition to the base camp of Mount Everest. Nobody believed he could achieve such a feat, and most believed he shouldn't attempt it. But Besecker did it anyway—not to prove them wrong but to show him-self, and the world, that when you're knocked down, you get back up . . . EVEREST STRONG.

Website: www.RobBesecker.com

 EverestStrongRB | EverestStrongRB | /in/Besecker

 EverestStrongRB

CPSIA information can be obtained
at www.ICGtesting.com
Printed in the USA
LVHW09*0309260818
588050LV00003B/9/P

9 780999 439401